Congress of Wo/men
Religion, Gender, and Kyriarchal Power

Elisabeth Schüssler Fiorenza

WIPF & STOCK · Eugene, Oregon

Wipf and Stock Publishers
199 W 8th Ave, Suite 3
Eugene, OR 97401

Congress of Wo/men
Religion, Gender, and Kyriarchal Power
By Schüssler Fiorenza, Elisabeth
Copyright © 2016 by Schüssler Fiorenza, Elisabeth All rights reserved.
Softcover ISBN-13: 978-1-6667-0418-1
Hardcover ISBN-13: 978-1-6667-0419-8
eBook ISBN-13: 978-1-6667-0420-4
Publication date 3/2/2021
Previously published by Dog Ear Publishing, 2016

With gratitude to my coworkers at FSR Inc.,
who through their labor and engagement have
sustained the work of *Feminist Studies in Religion*
over more than thirty years.

Contents

Contents

Acknowledgements

Many thanks to the Carter Center for its generous grant support of FSR Books toward publication of works that are consistent with the Carter Center's activities under its Human Rights Program and its Mobilizing Action for Women and Girls Initiative. To learn more about the Center's Forum on Women, Religion, Violence, and Power, visit: http://forumonwomen.cartercenter.org/#.

Each book has a special production history and unique "god-mothers" who have supported and watched over its birth in print. Hence, special thanks are due to my colleagues and friends, Dr. Melanie Johnson-DeBaufre, Dr. Kathryn Ott, and Midori Hartman, who have tirelessly worked to make this Feminist Studies in Religion book series possible. Melanie also has curated and shepherded *Congress of Wo/men* to publication. FSR Books student editors Elizabeth Freese and Nicole Hoskins have worked tirelessly to ensure the book's progress and success. Their collective advice and work were invaluable and I am deeply grateful for it.

Special thanks are also due to my research assistant Kelsi Morrison-Atkins, who not only read and corrected several drafts of all chapters but also corralled the contributions to the fourth chapter, edited it expertly. This student metalogue gathers the incisive and insightful discussions we had in my fall 2014 graduate seminar, Feminist Theories and The*logies, at Harvard University Divinity School. Kelsi's feedback improved not only my work but also that of her colleagues. I am also grateful to her for authoring the bibliography.

I was excited to learn that Dr. Heather Lee Miller, who has contributed to the *Journal of Feminist Studies in Religion* as expert copy editor for years, was able to copyedit this book, and with whom I enjoyed working greatly. Thanks, Heather, for your careful reading, clarifying suggestions, and painstaking work.

Thanks are due to the typesetter at Dog Ear Publishing.

This book has its roots and beginnings in the Cátedra MacKay lectures I gave in 2012 in Costa Rica, which were published in Spanish as "Poder, Diversidad y Religión," in a special issue of *La Revista Vida y Pensamiento*.[1] I want to thank Universidad Bíblica Latinoamericana, Costa Rica, especially Mireya Baltodano and Violeta Rocha, for facilitating my visit, as well as Ruth Mooney for translating and José Enrique Ramirez for publishing the lectures.

Last but not least, I want to thank all the coeditors, student coeditors, and managing editors of FSR Inc., with whom I have had the privilege to work over the last thirty years. I dedicate this book as a token of my gratitude to every one of them. Feminist Studies in Religion is flourishing and the *congress of wo/men* is realized daily in and through such engagement and work.

---

[1] Elisabeth Schüssler Fiorenza, "Poder, Diversidad y Religión," special issue, *La Revista Vida y Pensamiento* 32, no. 2 (2013), which retains the Spanish publication rights.

INTRODUCTION

Toward a Critical-Political Feminist Theory
and The*logy

L inda Zerilli, professor of political science at the University of
Chicago, opens her book *Feminism and the Abyss of Freedom* with
a reflection on what brought her to feminism, stating that "the radical demand for women's political freedom, the right to be a partici-
pant in public affairs . . . the feminist challenge to the androcentrism
of the public sphere and the constitution of alternative spaces of freedom is what captured and held my interest."[1] She goes on to say that
although she was fascinated by theoretical feminist debates on identity and subjectivity, their lack of a demand for the political freedom
that had inspired her to join the feminist intellectual movement made
her weary. As important as the struggles to overcome "the cultural
constraints of normative masculinity" and the destabilization of the
category of wo/man[2] as the subject of feminism were, she had trouble

---

[1] Linda M. G. Zerilli, *Feminism and the Abyss of Freedom* (Chicago: University of
Chicago Press, 2005), ix.

[2] In order to lift into consciousness the linguistic violence of so-called generic male-
centered language, I write the term *wo/men* with a slash and use the term *wo/men* and
not *men* in an inclusive way. I suggest that whenever you read "wo/men," you understand it in a generic sense. Wo/man includes man, she includes he, and female
includes male. To use *wo/men* as an inclusive generic term invites male readers to
learn how to think twice and to experience what it means not to be addressed specifically. Since, according to philosopher Ludwig Wittgenstein, the limits of language are
the limits of our world, such a change of language patterns is a very important step
toward realizing a new feminist consciousness. See my collection, *Changing Horizons:
Explorations in Feminist Interpretation* (Minneapolis, MN: Fortress, 2013), 20n5.

1

seeing "how [such changes] could possibly occur in the absence of the demand for freedom" as she understood it.[3] Hence, it seemed important for Zerilli to question the assumptions and frameworks underlying the feminist project of destabilization.

Like Zerilli, I became dedicated to feminism because of my political understanding of religious community and the commitment to changing its exclusionary teachings and structures. I became a feminist because I was attracted to feminism's political frame and power to change the religious space where I was at home, Catholicism, which has an explicitly hierarchal, monarchic, and kyriarchal structure.[4] When the women's liberation movement was emerging in the 1960s, Roman Catholicism faced increasing pressure from modernity and the ethos of democracy, which it had resisted until Vatican II and which reactionary forces have tried to undo ever since. Around this time, Mary Daly staged a famous exodus out of Memorial Church in Harvard Yard, which symbolized the virulent feminist debate that permeated discussions of the feminist movement in religion: whether to remain identified with organized religion or to leave it behind. It was the radical democratic visions of the "people of G*d,"[5] the "priesthood of believers," and "the poor (wo/men)," and that of "social justice" that spurred me to work to

---

[3] Zerilli, *Feminism and the Abyss of Freedom*, ix.

[4] I have introduced the analytical terms *kyriarchy/kyriocentrism*, which are derived from the Greek *kyrios* (emperor, lord, master, father, husband) in order to specify that in Western societies, the system of domination and exploitation is not just patriarchal but kyriarchal—that is, it is defined not only by gender but also by race, class, ethnicity, imperialism, and age. For more discussion, see the following chapter as well as my collection of essays, *Empowering Memory and Movement: Thinking and Working across Borders* (Minneapolis, MN: Fortress, 2013), 3n7.

[5] I write *the*logy* in this open form in order to avoid the gendering of G*d. The*logy* literally means "speaking about G*d" (in Greek, *theos* is the masculine grammatical form). Hence, Carol Christ has suggested that we use the noun *thealogy* (in Greek, *thea* is the feminine grammatical form, meaning Goddess) instead. However, her suggested language also reinscribes gender into the Divine. Hence, I have rewritten the masculine form of *theos* (God) with the asterisk (the*s/the*logy) in order to draw attention to the simultaneously linguistic and theoretical problem of naming the Divine. Since all Western languages, including Greek, Latin, and English, are gendered and use the masculine as the norm, I use the asterisk * to interrupt and make conscious this grammatically masculine or feminine determination of the Divine.

change structures of domination in church, religion, and society and not to submit to this either/or question of religious identity virulent in feminist debates at the time. Like Zerilli, I am moved less by theoretical questions of gender than by the political restrictions of the freedoms and well-being of poor and exploited wo/men. I also question those assumptions and frameworks underlying the feminist projects of destabilization that are disjointed from feminist political practices and movements.

A Critical Feminist Political Theory and The*logy of Liberation

First, I must admit that my preferred definition of feminism can be summed up by a well-known bumper sticker a friend gave me on my birthday years ago, which proclaims that "feminism is the radical notion that wo/men are people."[6] The tongue-in-cheek statement alludes to the US constitution's democratic assertion of "We the People" and thus insists that wo/men are fully entitled and responsible citizens not only in society but also in religion.

Consequently, one would assume that such politically oriented feminist theoretical endeavors—whether situated in society or religion—would be compelled to engage with each other both agonistically and collaboratively. However, if one surveys the feminist theoretical literature on gender and feminist political theory, this has rarely been the case. In dominant feminist political-theoretical discussions, the modern binary between secular and religious has not been sufficiently deconstructed. Because this binary has not been thoroughly problematized, hegemonic and feminist political theory continues to label kyriarchal structures of domination as "hierarchical" (in other words, as holy or sacred structures). Yet, the framework

---

[6] Cheris Kramarae and Paula Treichler formulated this definition. See my introduction to *Feminist Biblical Studies in the Twentieth Century: Scholarship and Movement* (Minneapolis. MN: Fortress, 2013), 4. For a discussion of Kramarae's work, see Karen A. Foss, Sonja K. Foss, and Cindy L. Griffin, *Feminist Rhetorical Theories* (Thousand Oaks, CA: Sage, 1999), 33–68.

undergirding neoliberal domination is no longer "sacred/holy" but based rather on neoliberal economic structures. Neoliberalism's vision of the new national and world order is "a vision of competition, inequality, market 'discipline,' public austerity, and 'law and order.'"[7] Hence, "hierarchy's" religious-the*logical roots and loss of the power of legitimization in modernity are overlooked and not subjected to critical reflection in critical feminist debates. Feminist political theory has not sufficiently explored whether and how hierarchy still shapes gradations of neoliberal kyriarchy, a concept I discuss further in Chapter 1.

This book seeks to explore not only political and religious structures of domination but also religious space within those structures as political feminist spaces for change and transformation. Its *topos* (from the Greek for "place"; i.e., "place to find something") *Congress of Wo/men* is not just of feminist interest, but its areas of concern are also frequent rhetorical *topoi* of discussion in print and electronic media as well as in political discourses and public debates, for example, the Religious Right's "war on wo/men." Hence, I approach this book, *Congress of Wo/men*, not simply in terms of academic wo/men's or gender studies but rather in terms of a critical feminist political theory and the*logy of liberation.

Although in recent years feminist studies has recognized religion as a powerful force, theoretical discussions[8] in the field rarely take notice of the tremendous theoretical work that feminist theoreticians

---

[7] Lisa Duggan. *The Twilight of Equality: Neoliberalism, Cultural Politics, and the Attack on Democracy* (Boston: Beacon, 2003), x.

[8] For the discussion of feminist studies in religion, see, among many others, Darlene M. Juschka, *Feminism in the Study of Religion: A Reader* (New York: Continuum, 2001); Melissa Raphael, *Introducing Thealogy: Discourse on the Goddess* (Cleveland, OH: Pilgrim, 2000); Musimbi R. A. Kanyoro, *Introducing Feminist Cultural Hermeneutics: An African Perspective* (Cleveland, OH: Pilgrim, 2002); Rita M. Gross and Rosemary Radford Ruether, *Religious Feminism and the Future of the Planet: A Buddhist-Christian Conversation* (New York: Continuum, 2001); Anne M. Clifford, *Introducing Feminist Theology* (Maryknoll, NY: Orbis, 2001); Susan Frank Parsons, *The Cambridge Companion to Feminist Theology* (New York: Cambridge University Press, 2002); Stephanie Y. Mitchem, *Introducing Womanist Theology* (Maryknoll, NY: Orbis, 2002); Rosemary Radford Ruether, ed., *Feminist Theologies: Legacy and Prospect* (Minneapolis, MN: Fortress, 2007); Marcella Althaus-Reid and Lisa Isherwood, *Controversies in*

in religion have done. In order to take this work into account, feminist sociopolitical studies should recognize feminist studies *in* religion and *feminist the*logy* as their conversation partners. In distinction to feminist studies *of* religion, which take religion as an object of study and are shaped by the theoretical frameworks of the study of religion, feminist studies *in* religion are situated within religion as a political space that fosters either radical democratic or kyriarchal practices and visions.

Since the study of religion objectifies religion as a field of critical investigation, it does not speak from within particular religions. However, a radical feminist critique of religion (i.e., one going to the kyriarchal roots of traditional religions), I argue, must come from within a particular religion if such a radical critique should not lead simply to the rejection of wo/men's religiosity as "false consciousness" or to an apologetics of the kyriarchal status quo in religion. In order to engender the transformation of kyriarchal societies and religions, I have argued elsewhere that a radical critique of religion must first be articulated as the*logical critique.[9]

According to philosopher Max Horkheimer, a critical theory must meet three criteria:

- First, it must be *explanatory*. That is, it must develop a theory of society that explains what is wrong. I have developed such a

---

Feminist Theology (Controversies in Contextual Theology) (London: SCM, 2007); Margaret D. Kamitsuka, *Feminist Theology and the Challenge of Difference* (New York: Oxford University Press, 2007); María Pilar Aquino and Maria José Rosado-Nunes, eds., *Feminist Intercultural Theology: Latina Explorations for a Just World* (Maryknoll, NY: Orbis, 2007); and especially, the roundtables in the *Journal of Feminist Studies in Religion*, which now approaches its thirtieth year of publication.

[9] See Elisabeth Schüssler Fiorenza, *In Memory of Her: A Feminist Theological Reconstruction of Christian Origins* (New York: Crossroad, 1983), Elisabeth Schüssler Fiorenza, *Discipleship of Equals: A Critical Feminist Ekklesia-logy of Liberation* (New York: Crossroad, 1993), Elisabeth Schüssler Fiorenza, *But She Said: Feminist Practices of Biblical Interpretation* (Boston: Beacon, 1992), Elisabeth Schüssler Fiorenza, *Wisdom Ways: Introducing Feminist Biblical Interpretation* (New York: Orbis, 2001), Elisabeth Schüssler Fiorenza, *Transforming Vision: Explorations in Feminist The*logy* (Minneapolis, MN: Fortress, 2011), and Elisabeth Schüssler Fiorenza, *Empowering Memory and Movement*. I am well aware that the term *the*logy* is Christian-centric and therefore often replaced with *spirituality*. Yet, spirituality has become equally or more problematic because it has become a consumer item in neoliberal societies.

theory by explicating the structures of domination not just in terms of patriarchal gender but also in terms of kyriarchal relations that are constituted by the intersection of racial, class, and gender and colonial and heterosexual relations of domination.[10]

- Second, critical theory must be *practical*. That is, it must identify the agents that seek to bring about change. I see the new social movements, in general, and the global feminist liberation movements, in particular, as such agents of change. Moreover, a critical feminist the*logy not only seeks to understand and explain religion but also to change its kyriarchal formations.

- Finally, a critical theory must be *normative*. That is, it has to articulate not only practical goals but also ethical norms and theoretical visions for a future free from domination. Feminism, in my view, is such a normative theory and knowledge.[11]

Religion and the*logy at their best cultivate the dream of a world without domination, poverty, and oppression—a dream of well-being and love, a dream that inspires all religions. This dream inscribed in religious scriptures becomes repeatedly incipient reality here and now through the struggles of sociopolitical-religious liberation movements. Feminism is such a sociopolitical movement and practice that works toward a world free from dehumanizing domination compelled by the dream of a renewed and different, domination-free world. Religious and Christian feminism in turn are empowered by the hope that such a world of well-being can become reality through Divine Spirit power and energy. Feminist religious movements and the*logy are future-oriented and enlivened by the power of their vision.

---

[10] For the explication of these terms, see my books *But She Said, Wisdom Ways, Discipleship of Equals, Transforming Vision*, and *Empowering Memory and Movement*.
[11] See Max Horkheimer, *Critical Theory* (New York: Herder, 1972), 188–243.

Critical feminist the*logies and studies in religion spell out political visions and hope. They seek to name the reality of wo/men's oppression, to encourage actions of empowerment and liberation, and again and again to articulate anew such a vision of well-being. In my view, feminist emancipatory theories and the*logies have a double task: On the one hand, they have to name, question, transcend, and theorize relations of domination and dehumanization. On the other hand, they should create spaces and opportunities for very different wo/men to move across religious and social borders in order to encounter one another, to join in solidarity with one another, and to harness their power of change. Social and religious liberation movements thus empower critical feminist theories and the*logies.

A critical feminist the*logy of liberation thus seeks to delineate the power of religion as not only a destructive but also an emancipatory force. In analyzing the power of religion, it seeks to engage the theoretical analytics of gender as well as an intersectional analytic of the overlapping structures of oppression that constitute the multiplicative kyriarchal interlacing of domination.[12] Such an intersectional the*logical analysis of religion from within is by definition also political.

Political Theory and Religion

The term *political* derives from the Greek word *polis*, which designates the democratic city-state. Greek democracy—the model for modern democracy—was traversed and limited by the intersecting structures of domination and exclusion that a feminist political analytic seeks to name and to change. Hence, a critical feminist political study of religion and the*logy has as its theoretical dialogue partner not only feminist gender studies but also critical political theory. Here, I find Zerilli's Arendtian theory of the political most compelling, since it also understands feminism as a

---

[12] For the development of intersectionality as a heuristic concept, see Patricia Hill Collins, *Fighting Words: Black Women and the Search for Justice* (Minneapolis: University of Minnesota Press, 1998).

> constructive world building practice that changes political freedom
> from the "I-will" to the "I-can" . . . I-can belongs to women neither
> as a sex nor gender, neither as a "natural" nor social group. I-can
> belongs rather to women as a political collectivity, and it obtains in
> the practice of speaking in women's name. . . . I-can is the nonsov-
> ereign freedom of feminists as citizens engaged in word and deed,
> who are committed to the irreducible non-natural basis of political
> membership.[13]

Political theorist Hannah Arendt traced the origins of the concept of
democracy to the ancient Greek *polis*, from which we derive the word
politics. In the ancient world, only elite men who had freed themselves
from working for the necessities of life could practice politics. The
Greek notion of democracy rested on the distinction between the private household, as the realm of necessity, and the public *polis* (the
state democracy), where free men discovered who they were and
established their individuality with the assistance of others. In contrast to the household, which was given over to necessity and economics, politics was the realm of freedom.[14]

What Arendt did not spell out was that only freeborn, propertied
male citizens could engage in politics. As heads of household with
freeborn wo/men, children, and slave wo/men subject to them, they
were called *kyrioi*. To name such a sociopolitical context of Christian
scriptures and the*logies adequately, I have coined the term *kyriarchy*
instead of the central feminist analytic category of *patriarchy*. *Kyriarchy*
denotes a gradated system of dominations, and derives from combin-
ing the Greek noun *kyrios* (Latin *dominus*)—the lord, slave master,

---

13 Zerilli, *Feminism and the Abyss of Freedom*, 180.
14 Hannah Arendt, *The Human Condition* (Chicago: University of Chicago Press,
1958); Regarding Hannah Arendt, see, for example, Seyla Benhabib, *The Reluctant
Modernism of Hannah Arendt* (Thousand Oaks, CA: Sage, 1996); Susan Bickford, *The
Dissonance of Democracy* (Ithaca, NY: Cornell University Press, 1996); John McGowan,
Hannah Arendt: An Introduction (Minneapolis: University of Minnesota Press, 1998);
Bonnie Honig, ed., *Feminist Interpretations of Hannah Arendt* (University Park: Pen-
nyslvania University Press, 1995); and especially, Christa Schnabl, *Hannah Arendts
Theorie des Handelns im Horizont der theologischen Ethik* (Frankfurt: P. Lang, 1999).

father, husband, propertied, educated, free male to whom all the members of the household were subordinated and by whom they were controlled—and the Greek verb *archein*, which means to rule, dominate, or control.[15]

The necessary realm of the household was also thus the realm of domination. Freedom in the classical, Western political sense was exercised by freeborn, propertied men only.[16] Only the *kyrios/dominus/gentleman/Herr* was truly a free citizen with power. Built on the subordination and enslavement of certain members of household and state, Western democracy (including American) imitates the kyriarchal structure of Greek democracy. Historically (and only until relatively recently), the perspectives of slave wo/men have been mostly silent in the historical record; however, the echoes of their voices have rung through the centuries, claiming freedom and well-being for all.

In the last three hundred years or more, wo/men, black people, workers, poor, and immigrant peoples have argued for full citizen rights. Such struggles for wo/men's rights over their bodies, families, and legal standing have again become virulent in recent years in the United States where the Democrats allegedly fight a "war against religion" and the Republicans legislate, especially on the state level, a "war against wo/men." The Roman Catholic bishops have gone so far as to claim that the Obama administration wages a war against religion with its demand for religiously affiliated institutions to cover the cost of birth control for wo/men and its refusal to tolerate discrimination on religious grounds. Meanwhile, Republican-controlled state governments repeatedly deny wo/men's reproductive rights and increasingly make decisions against wo/men's reproductive freedoms, which amounts to a real "war" on wo/men. To curtail wo/men's citizen rights to self-determination, Republican state legislatures in the United States, for example, have closed reproductive

---

[15] For further discussion, see Chapter 2.
[16] See Michael Welker, ed., *Quest for Freedom: Biblical-Historical-Contemporary* (Neukirchen-Vluyn: Neukirchener Verlag, 2015).

healthcare clinics, fashioned personhood amendments for fertilized eggs, and decided that life begins with fertilization.[17]

In short, the definition of feminism as "the radical notion that wo/men are people" is a political one that underscores that feminist struggles for full citizenship rights are ongoing. We do not yet live in a postfeminist world where—as is often alleged—wo/men have won equal rights and feminism has outlived its necessity. At the same time, this political bumper-sticker definition of feminism ironically emphasizes that at the beginning of the twenty-first century, feminism should be a commonsense notion. Wo/men are not ladies, wives, handmaids, seductresses, or beasts of burden but fully entitled and responsible decision-making citizens.

This political definition positions feminism within radical democratic movements and discourses that argue for the rights of all the people who are wo/men. It evokes memories of struggles for equal citizenship and decision-making powers in society and religion. According to this political definition of feminism, men can advocate feminism just as wo/men can be antifeminist. Feminism does not just pertain to gender but also to race, class, imperialism, and age discrimination. It is concerned with not only patriarchal but also kyriarchal elite male domination. Consequently, feminist the*logy has to focus on the kyriarchal power relations inscribed in religious language and in sacred scripture understood as the word of G*d.

A critical feminist political the*logy of liberation, therefore, has not only the deconstructive task of denaturalizing hegemonic kyriarchal gender relations but also the reconstructive task of envisioning a different world, society, and religious community free from domination.[18] Such a feminist world construction that seeks to

---

[17] See "About Us," Personhood, http://www.personhood.com/about.
[18] Elisabeth Schüssler Fiorenza, "Critical Feminist The*logy of Liberation: A Decolonizing Political The*logy," in *Political Theology. Contemporary Challenges and Future Directions*, ed. Francis Schüssler Fiorenza, Klaus Tanner, Michael Welker (Louisville, KY: Westminster John Knox, 2013), 23–36. For a review of feminist political the*logy, see Stefanie Schäfer-Bossert and Elisabeth Hartlieb, *Feministische Theologie-Politische Theologie: Entwicklungen und Perspektiven* (Sulzbach: Ulrike Helmer Verlag, 2012).

articulate alternatives to kyriarchal relations of domination has been partially realized in history in and through emancipatory radical democratic movements. Consequently, I have sought not only to theorize *kyriarchy* as an analytic heuristic concept that can articulate the multiplicative intersectionality of discourses and structures of domination, but also to envision the *ekklēsia* or the congress of wo/men, responsible for the *kosmopolis of wo/men* as such an alternative sociothe*logical imaginary theoretical space. Insofar as the radical democratic vision of the *ekklēsia*, or the congress of wo/men, which annunciates "the equal dignity and power of the many," to paraphrase Arendt, has been realized historically and practically only within and in spite of kyriarchal democracy, it is necessary to qualify the democratic term *ekklēsia*, meaning "congress" with wo/men. Such a marker is necessary as long as wo/men are not full decision-making citizens in society, the academy, and religious institutions. Congress of wo/men signifies that radical democratic equality has not yet been fully realized.

In short, critical feminist the*logies and studies in religion, I argue, need to work with a radical democratic rather than just an anthropological or normative cultural theory of society and religion.[19] They need to be aware of the rhetoricality of this theory and articulate its social location, epistemic interests, and practical functions for changing relations of domination. In order to sustain such a critical feminist theory of religion, I submit, feminist studies in religion need to remain *the*logical* in the broadest sense of the word. Feminist inquiry best locates itself *within* religion rather than constructing and objectifying religion as the other by making it an object of the scholarly, allegedly value-neutral gaze.

Such a critical feminist the*logy of liberation and emancipatory studies in religion presupposes a critical theory of religion that is explanatory, practical, normative, and self-reflexive. Rather

---

[19] See Elisabeth Schüssler Fiorenza, *Democratizing Biblical Studies: Toward an Emancipatory Educational Space* (Louisville, KY: Westminster John Knox, 2009).

than construct a model of progressivist development from dogmatic the*logy to the value-free, objectivist study of religion, I would argue that both the academic study of religion and Christian the*logy must be reconceptualized in rhetorical-feminist terms.[20] The strong positivist version of objectivity advocated by academic religious (and the*logical) studies needs to be problematized.

In order to avoid a positivist ethos, one needs to understand religion and the*logy not simply as objects of study but also as sites of struggle. Scholars always speak from within a communal-cultural religious tradition, even when we have consciously rejected it or have never formally been part of it. I do not want to suggest that in order to understand religion one must refer primarily to the testimony of believers. Rather, I want to make a critical hermeneutical point: In order to study religion or any other subject matter, one always already has a preunderstanding of the subject matter that one seeks to understand. Studies of symbolic universes and religious practices are always already situated within the framework of religion, insofar as they are shaped by their religious, intellectual, and communal-cultural traditions, even if they have rejected or claim to have surpassed them. There is no value-neutral scholarship. Scholarship is always already situated—religiously, socially, culturally, and politically. Hence, feminist studies in religion must become conscious of speaking *from within* a particular religious-cultural tradition or intellectual community to which feminist discourse is simultaneously both insider and outsider.

However, feminist discourses speak not only from within a particular cultural-religious community and context but also from within a particular cultural-political space. For instance, I have developed a critical feminist political the*logy in the US context, which is traversed by blatant racism toward the first African-American elected president and by legal sexism with respect to wo/men's reproductive

---

[20] See Elisabeth Schüssler Fiorenza, *Rhetoric and Ethic: The Politics of Biblical Studies* (Minneapolis, MN: Fortress, 1999).

citizen rights. State legislatures and candidates for Congress advocate a "human personhood" amendment, which argues that the paramount right to life is vested in each human being from the moment of fertilization (calculated two weeks prior to that fertilization) without regard to age, race, sex, health, function, or condition of dependency. The right to life is the paramount and most fundamental right of a person so defined.

This proposed amendment to the constitution would criminalize not only abortion but also some forms of birth control. Lynn M. Paltrow, lawyer and executive director of National Advocates for Pregnant Women, and Jeanne Flavin, sociology professor at Fordham University, have aptly recorded this situation in their *New York Times* op-ed. Paltrow and Flavin demonstrate that, because of the Republicans' success in the 2014 midterm election, the effort to ban abortion and establish "personhood" rights to fertilized eggs, embryos, and fetuses continues to gain ground. According to Paltrow and Flavin, "Such laws are increasingly being used as the basis for arresting women who have no intention of ending a pregnancy and for preventing women from making their own decisions about how they will give birth."[21]

The effects of these measures are shocking: In Washington, DC, a judge ordered a gravely ill twenty-seven-year-old woman to have a caesarean section, knowing that it could—and ultimately did—result in her and the baby's death. Not only are these measures costing wo/men their lives, but wo/men nationwide are also being accused of "attempted fetal homicide" for delaying caesarean sections or even falling down a flight of stairs. Wo/men with mental health issues are also victimized, as is demonstrated by the arrest and sentencing of a depressed South Carolina wo/man who attempted suicide, resulting in miscarriage. Florida hospitals have even held wo/men hostage in

---

[21] Lynn M. Paltrow and Jeanne Flavin, "Pregnant, and No Civil Rights," *New York Times*, November 7, 2014, http://www.nytimes.com/2014/11/08/opinion/pregnant-and-no-civil-rights.html.

an attempt to control the circumstances of their pregnancy, making it impossible for them to care for their children at home. Flavin and Paltrow assert forcefully:

> These are not isolated or rare cases. Last year, we published a peer-reviewed study documenting 413 arrests or equivalent actions depriving pregnant women of their physical liberty during the 32 years between 1973, when *Roe v. Wade* was decided, and 2005. . . . The principle at the heart of contemporary efforts to end legal abortion is that fertilized eggs, embryos, and fetuses are persons or at least have separate rights that must be protected by the state. In each of the cases we identified, this same rationale provided the justification for the deprivation of pregnant women's physical liberty, as well as of the right to medical decision making, medical privacy, and bodily integrity.[22]

Wo/men's citizen rights are jeopardized when everyone involved in abortions is criminalized. This law would also thereby create a new sizable prison population that would rob born children of their incarcerated mothers. Finally, the struggle for wo/men's reproductive rights has been declared a threat to "religious freedom" against which conservative church leaders, such as the Roman Catholic bishops, have been fighting for the continued right to discriminate and curtail wo/men's rights. How has feminist theory responded to this sociopolitical religiously supported discrimination against wo/men?

Mapping the Political Feminist Imagination

In a constructive article entitled "Mapping the Feminist Imagination" and more recently in her book *Fortunes of Feminism*, political theorist Nancy Fraser has sought to correct the standard feminist narrative of progress, according to which feminism has developed from

---

[22] Ibid.

an exclusionary white, middle-class, heterosexual woman-dominated movement to a broader movement that allows for the inclusion of the needs of lesbians, working-class, migrant, and poor wo/men as well as wo/men of color.[23]

Fraser is critical of this standard feminist narrative not only because it is modernist and progressivist but also because it tells the story of feminist theory and movement as an internal development without making connections to broader sociopolitical developments. Fraser seeks to make such connections when she reconstructs three phases in the trajectory of second-wave feminism. Second-wave feminism's first phase, which Fraser characterizes as "redistribution" of social power and economic resources, began as one of the New Left and Civil Rights social movements that sought to engender a "socialist imaginary" and an "expanded idea of social equality," arguing for justice and equal rights and presupposing the welfare state and social democracy. This phase sought for the social and economic well-being of wo/men.

The second phase, which Fraser terms "recognition," sought acknowledgment of cultural differences. This phase, which coincided with postcommunism and postcolonialism, was dedicated to bringing about cultural change and transformation. Cultural change and recognition were always an important project of feminism but were now decoupled from the project of distributive justice and political-economic transformation. In the context of the right-wing, political, monocapitalist developments of the mid-1980s and 1990s, she says,

> The turn to recognition dovetailed all too neatly with a hegemonic neoliberalism that wanted nothing more than to repress all memory of social egalitarianism. The result was a tragic historical irony.

---

[23] Nancy Fraser, "Mapping the Feminist Imagination: From Redistribution to Recognition to Representation," *Constellations* 12, no. 3 (2005): 295–307. For a fuller development of her argument, see also Nancy Fraser, "Identity, Exclusion, and Critique: A Response to Four Critics," *European Journal of Political Theory* 6, no. 3 (2007): 305–38, and Nancy Fraser, *Fortunes of Feminism: From State-Managed Capitalism to Neoliberal Crisis* (London: Verso, 2013).

Instead of arriving at a broader, richer paradigm that could encompass both redistribution and recognition, we effectively traded one truncated paradigm for another—a truncated economism for a truncated culturalism.[24]

The third emerging phase of the feminist imaginary has been that of a transnational politics of "representation," which seeks to link and integrate the economic politics of redistribution and the cultural politics of recognition within a transnational frame.[25] Since transnational misdistribution, misrecognition, and misrepresentation cannot be adequately addressed in a state-territorial frame, transnational feminist theory has to reframe the problem of meta-injustice in a global context. Fraser understands "representation" as "claims-making" in political terms, not only as ensuring equal political voice for wo/men in national communities but also, and most important, in the transnational arena.

The post-9/11 political situation in the United States, which has far-reaching implications for global capitalism, Fraser suggests, is characterized by the strategy of a "gender-coded politics of recognition" invoked to "hide a regressive politics of economic redistribution."

---

[24] Fraser, "Mapping," 299. The narrative of progress has been widely critiqued in postcolonial studies. See, for example, Anne McClintock, *Imperial Leather: Race, Gender, and Sexuality in the Colonial Contest* (London: Routledge, 1995), and Anne McClintock, Aamir Mufti, and Ella Shohat, eds., *Dangerous Liaisons: Gender, Nation, and Postcolonial Perspectives* (Minneapolis: University of Minnesota Press, 1997).

[25] Since Fraser is concerned with political misrepresentation but not with linguistic misrepresentation as "representing" wo/men in writing and research, she does not refer to the intense discussions on the "politics of representation" of white Western feminists, whose cultural studies writings "represent" third-world wo/men as passive victims. For this discussion, see especially Gayatri Chakravorty Spivak, "Can the Subaltern Speak?" in *Marxism and the Interpretation of Culture*, ed. Cary Nelson and Lawrence Grossberg (Urbana: University of Illinois Press, 1988), 271–97; and Chandra Talpade Mohanty, "Under Western Eyes," in *Third World Wo/men and the Politics of Feminism*, ed. Chandra Talpade Mohanty, Ann Russo, and Lourdes Torres (Bloomington: Indiana University Press, 1991), 51–80. Fraser's concern is clearly with "challenging the state-territorial framing of political claims making" (ibid., 51). To that end, she also argues that the center of feminist action in this third phase is no longer the West (i.e., the United States and Europe) but wo/men's movements around the world.

Both in the rhetoric of the "war on terror" as well as in the "family-values" campaign, especially with regard to abortion rights and same-sex marriage, the manipulation of gender has been, according to Fraser, "a crucial instrument of Bush's victory" in the 2004 election. This victory was achieved through the alliance of "free-marketeers" with Christian "fundamentalists."

The capitalist politics of regressive economic redistribution manipulated immigration, race, and gender codes and used antifeminist politics of recognition "to conceal an anti-working class politics of regressive redistribution"—a politics that creates the social "insecurity society" as a successor to the welfare society.[26] In a time when people experience real economic and social insecurities, religious fundamentalism, in general, and Christian evangelicalism, in particular, can palliate pervasive anxiety. However, they do not actually give people security but provide means to cope with such insecurity. With reference to Michel Foucault, Fraser understands evangelicalism "as a care-of-self-technology that is especially suited to neo-liberalism, insofar as the latter is always generating insecurity."[27] She concludes that many working-class wo/men "are deriving something significant from evangelicalism, something that confers meaning on their lives."[28]

This situation of working-class wo/men requires reframing disputes about injustice, which seeks to change the framework from one focused on nation states or territories to one with global reach. Thus, transnational feminism is in the process "of reconfiguring gender justice as a three-dimensional problem, in which redistribution, recognition, and representation must be integrated in a balanced way . . . to challenge the full range of gender injustices in a globalized world."[29]

---

[26] Fraser, "Mapping," 301.

[27] Ibid., 303.

[28] Ibid. However, she concludes that feminists have not yet "figured out how to talk to them or what feminism can offer them in its place." This remark reveals not only ignorance by a leading feminist theorist of the feminist work done in religion and the*logy but also the assumption that feminism can be substituted for religion.

[29] Ibid., 305.

In the process of being reconfigured, the three successive, overlapping stages of feminist political struggles and their theoretical deliberations become three dimensions of the problem that transnational feminist theory and politics face today.

This reconfiguration is important because it seeks to overcome the developmental rhetoric of three phases. Such reframing also recognizes the

> intricate imbrications of relations of race, gender, sexuality and class in the institutions of capitalist modernity. As a historical matter, status and class are not separated by capitalism, which operates through status categories at every stage of its historical development. Status and class are rhetorically disarticulated (in the U.S. this occurs through the early decades of the nineteenth century) in order to remove capitalism from the demands of even a limited, purely formal democracy of white men.[30]

Fraser's mapping of the "feminist imagination" also opens up a theoretical space for mapping transnational feminist studies in religion.[31] With Fraser, I suggest that a transnational decolonizing the*logy also needs to articulate three dimensions: historical redistribution, ideological deconstruction, and ethical—political as well as religious—the*logical constructive representation, which requires a reframing of feminist studies in religion so that they can "challenge the full range of injustices in the world," while at the same time articulating "technologies of the self " (Foucault) that inspire wo/men to struggle for survival and transformation.

Following Fraser's model, I argue that whereas the first phase of second-wave feminism the*logy sought to "write wo/men back into

---

[30] Duggan, *Twilight of Equality*, 83–84.
[31] See Elisabeth Schüssler Fiorenza, "The Power of the Word: Charting Critical Global Feminist Biblical Studies," in *Feminist New Testament Studies: Global and Future Perspectives*, eds. Kathleen O'Brien Wicker, Althea Spencer Miller, and Musa W. Dube (New York: Palgrave MacMillan, 2005), 43–62.

history" and into the sociopolitical Christian imagination, the second phase has laid bare the ideological mechanisms of kyriocentric texts and kyriarchal institutional practices, with the dangerous potential of yet again moving embodied historical wo/men to the margins of the theoretical gaze. The third mode in turn seeks to integrate redistribution and ideological recognition with representation by reframing feminist studies in the*logy and religion so that they can speak to the "care of the self" as well as to inspiring transreligious emancipatory actions for change.

We need to reframe Scripture and the*logical studies in such a way that we can both analyze, for instance, the struggles of wo/men in the Roman Empire and make political-religious connections to the struggles, interests, and aspirations of wo/men for survival and justice today, in a global empire that makes life increasingly poorer and more insecure for the majority of people. However, we need to be careful to understand Fraser's proposal not as three sequential steps but as a dynamic model defined by simultaneity.

We can do so, I suggest, by carefully analyzing and reframing the workings of power in the religious discourses of the past and those of the present as well as by constructing an imaginative space for articulating an alternative radical egalitarian discursive imagination. Hence, I invite readers to engage my reflections with this theoretical framework in mind. While particular geographical or identity-centered articulations of feminist the*logy are important, we also need to take into account our commonality in a neoliberal empire that shapes our present cultural-political religious situations around the globe.[32]

Globalization and Feminist Movements

The common sociopolitical space of all feminist theories and the*logies is neoliberal *globalization*. *The Oxford Handbook of Feminist Theology* characterizes this common sociopolitical location as follows:

---

[32] Such as European, Asian, African, South American, Mesoamerican, North American, or Oceanian.

This *Handbook* tries to present an inclusive account of feminist theology in the early twenty-first century that acknowledges the reflection of women on religion beyond the global North and its forms of
Christianity. It has, therefore, chosen globalization as its central
theme, as the foremost characteristic of the context in which we do
feminist theology today. . . . For feminist theology to take seriously
the enormously complex topic of globalization requires that it move
beyond its basic narrative as a movement defined by the USA.[33]

While I agree with this diagnosis of the setting and location of feminist
the*logy in the twenty-first century, I do not want to reduce feminist
the*logy and studies in religion to a "reflection of wo/men on religion"
nor do I think that globalization challenges narratives of feminist
the*logy. Rather, with feminist scholar María Pílar Aquino, I want to
argue that we should not "rethink feminist theology in light of globalization" but rather "rethink globalization in light of critical feminist liberation theology. What is in question is not the relevance of this theology,
but the model of society that today's globalization is creating. The challenge facing any feminist theology lies in rethinking what it has to do for
intervening in the redesign of this model in the coming decades."[34]
Aquino argues that "globalization interprets society as grounded on the
social forces that make up the capitalist market" and "work toward the
imposition of the market model on a global scale."[35] She goes on to characterize kyriarchal globalization thus:

- Neither the two-thirds of humanity living in poverty nor the
  vast majority of wo/men living in subordination, poverty, and
  violence but the financial and political elites benefit from
  globalization.

---

[33] Sheila Briggs and Mary McClintock Fulkerson, eds., "Introduction," in *Oxford Handbook of Feminist Theology*, eds. Mary McClintock Fulkerson and Sheila Briggs (New York: Oxford University Press, 2011), 2.
[34] María Pílar Aquino, "Theology and Identity in the Context of Globalization," in Fulkerson and Briggs, *Oxford Handbook of Feminist Theology*, 422.
[35] Ibid.

- The ideology of kyriarchal globalization idealizes and transforms the capitalist market into a being that provides "capital as a source of life, endorses profit as the supreme value" and also promises "endless progress, without any concern for environmental justice."
- This vision of society is not based on the recognition of and respect for human rights but on the unrestricted expansion of the capitalist market. It denies human rights to wo/men in the interests of kyriarchal family and culture.
- The world capitalist globalization creates in the twenty-first century is marked by "violent conflict, political tension, and human insecurity in every continent." Most of the conflicts have been sparked "by issues of ethnic identity and religion, combined with systemic factors linked to social injustice, long standing hatreds, or demands caused by human needs not being met."[36]

All these characteristics of capitalist globalization are, for instance, on display in the present US political situation. Politically conservative voices defend the military-industrial complex and refuse to tax the profits of the super-rich while at the same time they diminish and deconstruct the social net the "welfare state" provides. Republican-controlled state legislatures seek in various ways to curtail the democratic election rights of poor, young, old, and minority voters. The Supreme Court has declared that corporations, like people, have the right to free speech, a decision that has resulted in millions of dollars paid for election advertisements seeking to make manifold profit by electing what amounts to a corporate conservative president. Poor wo/men not only in the United States but also around the world who are denied means of birth control and abortions suffer the brand of this anti-wo/man politics of globalization.

---

[36] Ibid., 423–28.

Whereas Aquino insists on the negative, destructive aspects of globalization, Valentine Moghadam argues in *Globalization and Social Movements* that globalization is a "multifaceted process of social change" that has negative and positive effects: *globalization from above* and *globalization from below*.[37]

> Globalization in its neoliberal capitalist form is called *"globalization-from-above."* It is the latest stage of capitalism on a world scale, involving the spread of neoliberal capitalism through investment, trade, and war. . . . Given the capitalist bases of globalization, the inequalities of class, gender, and race are maintained through processes of accumulation and patterns of distribution in the productive, reproductive, and virtual economies within and across the core, periphery, and semi-periphery of the world system.[38]

Globalization-from-above is characterized by hypermasculinity expressed in militarism, corporate exploitation, sexual conquest, religious fanaticism, and emphasized femininity "constructed around adaptations to male power."[39] Transnational social movements characterized by mass mobilization uniting people in three or more countries constitute globalization-from-below. Both transnational social movements and transnational advocacy networks are linked to globalization but in somewhat different ways. They are enabled by increasing usage of the Internet, mobile phones, blogs, and social network media such as Facebook and Twitter. The principal conviction that inspires these movements and networks is the belief that "another world is possible" as well as the conviction "that we are all human beings first, and privileged with responsibilities to each other, to future generations, and to the planet."[40]

---

[37] Valentine M. Moghadam, *Globalization and Social Movements: Islamism, Feminism, and the Global Justice Movement*, 2nd ed. (Lanham, MD: Rowman & Littlefield, 2013).
[38] Ibid., 27.
[39] Ibid., 52.
[40] Ibid., 9.

Moghadam focuses on and discusses three transnational social movements that emerged under the conditions of neoliberal globalization: the political Islamist movement, the wo/men's or feminist movement, and the global justice movement, which are similar but not interchangeable. Whereas Islamist movements seek state power, feminist global justice movements pursue wide-ranging "institutional and normative changes and eschew violence."[41]

Transnational feminism emerged as focusing and organizing around issues of neoliberal globalization. Mary Hawkesworth has defined global feminist activism as international feminist mobilization involving wo/men in more than one country and region "who seek to forge a collective identity among women and improve the conditions of women."[42] This does not mean that transnational feminisms speak with one voice. Rather, in the interest of feminist activism and the analysis of different contexts, they seek to negotiate differences in their own ranks or with respect to other groups within an overall frame of opposition to neoliberal globalization. In Moghadam's view, the wo/men's liberation movement emerged in the 1960s and 1970s within national borders, but since the mid-1980s, transnational feminist movements materialized because of transnational economic and political developments.[43]

To sum up this argument:

- With the transition from Keynesian to neoliberal economic policy and the "feminization of labor"[44] as its consequence in the mid-1980s, a shift took place in the form of bridge- and consensus-building across regional and ideological divides. The result of this globalizing economic development was that wo/men comprised nearly half of the world's labor force in the

---

[41] Ibid., 13.

[42] Mary E. Hawkesworth, *Globalization and Feminist Activism* (Lanham, MD: Rowman & Littlefield, 2006), 27.

[43] Moghadam, *Globalization and Social Movements*, 133–70.

[44] Guy Standing, "Global Feminization through Flexible Labor," *World Development* 17, no. 7 (1989): 1077–95 and *World Development* 27, no. 3 (1999): 583–602.

1990s but received low wages and struggled with poor working conditions in addition to their traditional household work.

- Privatization and denationalization of the labor markets and depletion of the public sector workforce led to the feminization of poverty.
- The rise of various forms of fundamentalism put pressure on states to enforce traditional family norms, tighten control over wo/men, and curtail wo/men's rights. As a consequence, groups of transnational feminisms emerged to defend wo/men's human rights, gender justice, and gender equality; and to work against the feminization of poverty, violence against wo/men, and wo/men's rights abuses such as systemic rape, sexual slavery, and forced pregnancy.
- Mounting militarism and violence reactivated wo/men's long-standing engagement for peace, which sought to "engender" nuclear disarmament, peace and human rights, and reintegration of former combatants and displaced persons, involving wo/men in peace negotiations, antiwar protests, and feminist humanitarianism.

In contrast to the oppressive effects of "globalization from above," transnational feminist networks are representative of the enactment of the alternative "globalization from below" insofar as they have overcome the wo/men's movement's North-South antagonisms by adopting the following strategies of

- creating, activating, or joining global networks;
- participating in multilateral and intergovernmental public arenas;
- acting within states to enhance public awareness of social policies or military issues;
- networking with each other by inter-networking and especially Internet-working, which allows feminist advocacy and activist networks to operate in local, national, regional, and global terrains.

To bring about change, feminist transnational networks have developed resonant theoretical-practical frames that inspire and motivate working wo/men cross-culturally and around the globe. These frames include wo/men's empowerment and wo/men's human rights, including reproductive rights, gender equality, and gender justice. In short, transnational feminist networks have been successful because their "politics is goal directed rather than identity based."[45]

This account of the process of alternative globalization-from-below raises the question of why feminist the*logy and studies in religion have remained stuck in the identity politics of the 1980s, replicating again and again the North-South or first-world/two-thirds world rhetoric rather than creating global transconfessional or transreligious networks and articulating common goals. Why do we apply the white supremacist racist labels of the North-South or first-world/two-thirds world to feminist work if such work is liberationist, critically analyzing and rejecting racist prejudice? Without question, it is appropriate to do so if feminist work is white racist and does not critically reflect on white privilege, but should all feminist work that is articulated by Euro-American, Australian, African, South American, and Mesoamerican authors of European descent be so labeled? One of the reasons for such divisive identity politics seems to be engendered by the increasing location of feminist studies in the*logy and religion in the academy's competitive ethos and neoliberal practices.[46]

If neoliberal globalization engenders fundamentalist movements around the globe, then feminist the*logy and studies in religion have to move beyond discussing identity politics to elaborating religiously and the*logically the transnational feminist theoretical-practical frames that inspire and motivate wo/men cross-culturally

---

[45] Ibid., 170.
[46] See Lee Hall, "I Am an Adjunct Professor Who Teaches Five Classes and I Earn Less than a Pet-Sitter," *The Guardian*, June 23, 2015, http://www.alternet.org/education/i-am-adjunct-professor-who-teaches-five-classes-and-i-earn-less-pet-sitter?akid=13239.309111.KKXjxm&rd=1&src=newsletter1038286&t=15, according to which 76 percent of instructional staff appointments in US higher education are now not even full-time jobs.

and around the globe. We need to develop theoretical frames and organizational strategies that focus on global issues of wo/men's rights and justice and not only articulate them in religious-the*logical frames but also explore them in terms of sacred scriptures and religious traditions. This will require a much closer collaboration among scholars and ministers or religious leaders and community builders.

An examination of neoliberal capitalist globalization thus calls for a critical feminist analysis and for organizing global feminist transconfessional movements of conscientization in religion. It calls for a reorientation of feminist the*logy and studies in religion toward their roots in the wo/men's liberation movements around the globe. Feminist the*logies and studies in religion need to test and evaluate postmodern feminist theories and malestream scholarship in terms of the struggles against the devastating consequences of capitalist globalization and in support of global feminist movements that struggle for the well-being of everyone without exception and for the flourishing of the planet.

I recognize the important tools postmodern deconstruction has given us in order to interrogate the forms of knowledge that reproduce stereotyping forms of power and pervasive ideologies of kyriarchal domination in language that colonizes the imagination. However, I disagree with the totalizing deployment of this approach, which tells us that there is no way to escape either the self-referential system of language or the powers of exploitation in order to produce knowledge that is transformative.[47] Hence, I insist that we need to engage in not only deconstruction and critical struggle but also reconstructing and revisioning, articulating methods and practices of dekyriarchalizing the imagination, deimperializing scripture and the*logy, and decolonizing the Divine.

---

[47] See also Leela Fernandes, *Transforming Feminist Practice: Non-Violence, Social Justice, and the Possibility of a Spiritualized Feminism* (San Francisco: Aunt Lute, 2003). While I agree with her critique of secularized feminism, and her attempt to reclaim the sacred for feminism, I do not think this can be or should be accomplished by spiritualizing feminism.

Historically, the language of democracy, equality, and justice articulated in different cultural and religious "tongues" has provided an alternative imaginary space to kyriarchal imperialism. Although democracy has different shades of meaning in different historical contexts that are not always liberating, "democracy through the times has been and still is the discourse that sets the terms for critique of current affairs and institutional orders and creates the basis for their change."[48] Radical democracy, which I have religiously articulated as the *ekklēsia of wo/men* responsible for the *kosmopolis of wo/men*, offers the language and space for the imagination to develop public religious discourses "wherein justice, participation, difference, freedom, equality, and solidarity set the ethical conditions."[49]

The challenge today then seems to be whether in and through the deconstruction of kyriarchal inscriptions of biblical and the*logical discourses we can articulate an alternative religious imagination different from that of the imperial imaginary of traditional Christianity. Since Christian fundamentalisms draw on the kyriarchal language of empire inscribed in the Bible and tradition, must feminist the*logy and studies in religion also draw on scripture for reconstructing a radical democratic egalitarian vision also inscribed in Christian scriptures and traditions? This is not just a question for Christian and other scholars of religion but for all who seek transformative practices of imagination and vision that can articulate radical democratic discourses inspired by sacred scriptures and traditions of the world.

At the time of this writing, the neoliberal American kyriarchal democracy displays increasingly fascistic elements, which Christian religious language often further sanctions. Poverty engendered by neoliberalism, the displacement of entire nations through military conflict, the global slave trade, permanent war against terrorism, and the ever-expanding "war on wo/men" constitute the horizon of

---

[48] Adriana Hernández, *Pedagogy, Democracy, and Feminism: Rethinking the Public Sphere* (New York: SUNY Press, 1997), 31.
[49] Ibid., 32.

feminist thought and struggles not only in society but also in religion. Hence, the quest for ethical and religious feminist political visions and movements for justice becomes more and more pressing. In this book, I seek to address these problems by following Fraser's lead and addressing all three components of the development in feminist political theory: the sociopolitical, poststructuralist deconstructive, and kosmo-political phase of feminism as interconnected and dynamic intellectual feminist theoretical spaces.

Chapter 1 discusses kyriarchal power and how the scriptural "power of the word" still affects the life of wo/men around the world. Chapter 2 explores the question of diversity in critical discussion with "New Feminism," the feminine genius, or "emphasized femininity," constructed around adaptation to hypermasculinity and kyriarchal power. I focus on two Christian essentialist gender identity constructs of "woman," and "the feminine" and the ways in which they function to co-opt and exclude wo/men at one and the same time. Such analysis comes to light with the conceptual framework of kyriarchy as a system of intersecting pyramidal power structures of race, class, gender, religion, culture, and corporality, which encompasses sex, disability, age, color, and other bodily markers.

Chapter 3 seeks to explore the theoretical and spiritual Christian visions that enable us to question, resist, and change kyriarchal relations of global domination. As one such utopian imaginary, I propose the notion of the *ekklēsia of wo/men*, conceptualized as the radical democratic assembly of the *kosmopolis*, *basileia*, or *G*d's other world*. G*d's different *kosmopolis* is envisioned here as an alternative imaginative space to the so-called global village capitalist neoliberalism has created. The arguments of the first three chapters foreground the analytic concept of kyriarchy and its alternative, the *kosmopolis*, in order to analyze and reenvision the kind of power religion and sacred scriptures legitimate.

Chapter 4 is not a conclusion but a dialogue among young feminist thinkers who will define future feminist the*logy or studies in religion and enact feminist transformations in different spaces and locations. Rather than calling this last chapter an "epilogue," which usually consists of a summary and conclusion, we have decided to develop it as a "metalogue," a conversation about a theoretical subject such as can be found in my *Democratizing Biblical Studies*.[50]

This "roundtable metalogue" situates the book's argument in conversation with other feminist theoretical voices—my students and the readers of this book. Participants in the roundtable approached the overall topic from different thematic and methodological angles. They not only theorize justice and well-being but also organize and elaborate existing critical cosmopolitan feminist places or interconnected global intellectual spaces for feminist studies and struggles that do not exclude religion but seek to transform it. In short, the last chapter moves from feminist theory in an authorial mode to dialogical experiences and practices expressed in different voices and perspectives. Hence, it presents a collaborative effort to reflect on the book's topics through emergent feminist voices seeking to continue its dialogues with you, the reader. I hope that not only readers of this book but future contributors to the book series in feminist studies in religion that this book inaugurates will continue the conversation we started in the seminar.

---

[50] See Elisabeth Schüssler Fiorenza, *Democratizing Biblical Studies: Toward an Emancipatory Educational Space* (Louisville, KY: Westminster John Knox, 2009), 169–206.

CHAPTER 1

The Violence of Kyriarchal Power

I n *Why Stories Matter: The Political Grammar of Feminist Theory*, Clare Hemmings reminds us that it matters how we tell our stories and histories of feminism.[1] Women's studies scholars began by naming the oppressive powers at work in our world as *patriarchy*, which literally means "the rule of the father of the household" but was generally understood as the domination of men over wo/men. Since around the beginning of the 1980s, patriarchy as a key subject of feminist analysis has been replaced, however, by gender.[2] It is important to note that gender studies arrived on the scene at the same time as neoliberal economic globalization, and its academic discourses gained ground around the world.[3] The service industry of neoliberal globalization has not only exploited wo/men globally but also

---

[1] Clare Hemmings, *Why Stories Matter: The Political Grammar of Feminist Theory* (Durham, NC: Duke University Press, 2011). See also Ann Oakley, *Sex, Gender, and Society* (New York: Harper & Row, 1972); Rosemary Radford Ruether, "Patriarchy," in *An A to Z of Feminist Theology*, eds. Lisa Isherwood and Dorothea McEwan (Sheffield: Sheffield Academic Press, 1996), 173–74; and Sylvia Walby, *Theorizing Patriarchy* (Oxford: Basil, 1990). See, for example, Ernst Bornemann, *Das Patriarchat—Ursprung und Zukunft unseres Gesellschaftssystems* (Frankfurt am Main: Fischer, 1991); Maria Mies, *Patriarchy and Accumulation on a World Scale: Women in the International Division of Labour* (New York: Palgrave, 1999); Lorraine Code, "Patriarchy," in *Encyclopedia of Feminist Theories*, ed. Lorraine Code (London: Routledge, 2000), 378–79; and Pierre Bourdieu, *Masculine Domination*, trans. Richard Nice (Stanford, CA: Stanford University Press, 2001).

[2] See Mary Holmes, *What Is Gender? Sociological Approaches* (Thousand Oaks, CA: Sage, 2007).

reduced the economic power of working- and middle-class white men to that of working-class and racialized wo/men, while simultaneously promoting an ethos of aggressive masculinity.

Thus, this transition from women's studies to gender studies is, according to Hemmings, "more likely institutionally supported where it is harnessed to globalization and seen as producing future gender mainstreaming or gender and development experts."[4] Attention to this transition story from women's and feminist studies to gender studies would bring into question Nancy Fraser's argument that feminism has made three major contributions to the neoliberal ethos: questioning the "family wage, " promoting identity politics, and embracing NGOs.[5]

Contrary to Fraser, one could argue that it was not feminism but the Western dualistic "masculine-feminine" framework of gender that harnessed women's studies to neoliberal globalization.[6] Economic status has, therefore, not been "equalized" by the feminist campaign for equal pay and work conditions, but rather neoliberalism has equalized the economic status of working-class men with that of working-class, single mothers and poor wo/men, who could never rely on a "family wage."[7] Hence, it is important to tell the story of feminist theory and the*logy with respect to neoliberalism. As feminist theorist Clare Hemmings has argued, whatever stories we tell about the feminist past will shape our visions for its future.[8]

---

[3] See David Harvey, *A Brief History of Neoliberalism* (Oxford: Oxford University Press, 2005).

[4] Hemmings, *Why Stories Matter*, 10–11.

[5] Nancy Fraser, "How Feminism Became Capitalism's Handmaiden and How to Reclaim It," *The Guardian*, October 14, 2013, http://theguardian.com/commentisfree/2013/oct/14/feminism-capitalist-handmaiden-neoliberal?CMP=twt_gu.

[6] For the affinity of neoliberalism to totalitarianism see Henry A. Giroux, "Donald Trump and the Ghost of Totalitarianism," September 9, 2015, http://www.tikkun.org/nextgen/donald-trump-and-the-ghost-of-totalitarianism.

[7] Fraser, "How Feminism Became Capitalism's Handmaiden."

[8] In addition to Hemmings, see Andrea Cornwall, Jasmine Gideon, and Kalpana Wilson, "Introduction: Reclaiming Feminism: Gender and Neoliberalism," *IDS Bulletin* 39, no. 6 (2008): 1–9; Rahila Gupta, "Has Neoliberalism Knocked Feminism Sideways?" *50.50 Inclusive Democracy*, January 4, 2012, https://www.opendemocracy.net/5050/rahila-gupta/has-neoliberalism-knocked–feminism-sideways; and Mary Evans, "Feminism and the Implications of Austerity," *Feminist Review* 109 (2015): 146–55.

Gender[9]

The history of gender studies is not just a story important for feminism in the West but rather a story of global dimensions. In the 1970s, women's studies introduced the distinction between social gender roles and biological sex. By the mid-1980s, gender studies emerged alongside women's studies as a distinct field of inquiry. Gender theory questions seemingly universal beliefs about wo/men and men and attempts to unmask the cultural, societal, and political roots of gender. Women's studies scholars first objected to the introduction of this analytic category because it no longer articulated that *wo/men as historical agents* were the focal point of feminist analysis.

Moreover, by replacing the central analytic feminist categories of *patriarchy* and *androcentrism* (male-centered ideology) with *gender*, the question of power relations was muted and often eclipsed, since in distinction to the categories of patriarchy and androcentrism, gender no longer articulates relations of power. Gender has become a key analytic category alongside race, class, age, colonialism, and other identity markers, a development that has led to an "adding up of oppressions" working alongside each other and constituting different dualistic frameworks of analysis.[10] This dualistic gender analytic has

---

[9] Conversation partners in this chapter are also Marjorie Agosín, ed., *Women, Gender, and Human Rights: A Global Perspective* (New Brunswick, NJ: Rutgers University Press, 2001); Dennis Baron, *Grammar and Gender* (New Haven, CT: Yale University Press, 1986); Hadumond Bussmann and Renate Hof, eds., *Genus. Geschlechterforschung/Gender Studies in den Kultur- und Sozialwissenschaften. Ein Handbuch* (Stuttgart: A. Kröner Verlag, 2005); Judith Butler, *Gender Trouble: Feminism and the Subversion of Identity* (New York: Routledge, 1990); Judith Butler, *Undoing Gender* (New York: Routledge, 2004); Teresa De Lauretis, *Technologies of Gender* (Bloomington: Indiana University Press, 1987); bell hooks, *Yearning: Race, Gender, and Cultural Politics* (Boston, MA: South End, 1990); Judith Lorber, *Paradoxes of Gender* (New Haven, CT: Yale University Press, 1990); Stephen D. Moore and Janice Capel Anderson, eds., *New Testament Masculinities*, Semeia Studies (Atlanta: SBL, 2003); and Elisabeth Schüssler Fiorenza, "Gender, Sprache, und Religion: Feministisch–Theologische Anfragen," *Erträge. 60 Jahre Augustana* (Neuendettelsau: Augustana Hochschule e.V., 2008), 83–90.

[10] See the excellent and clear contribution of Barbara J. Riesman, "Gender as Social Structure: Theory Wrestling with Activism," in *The Kaleidoscope of Gender: Prisms, Patterns, and Possibilities*, eds. Joan Z. Spade and Catherine G. Valentine (Sage, 2007), 9–21.

also constituted the notion of *diversity* as the aggregation of such dualistic identity markers.

Originally, the word *gender* was a grammatical category of analysis. It derives from the Latin *gener* (genus, birth, race, kind, gender) and has traditionally referred to a grammatical feature of Indo-European languages that classifies nouns, pronouns, and modifiers in arbitrary groupings (masculine, feminine, and neuter). A more recent meaning of the word associates or equates it with biological sex and uses it as a functionalist social category of analysis.

Sex and Gender as Sociopolitical Constructs

In Western societies, only two genders—male and female—are thought to exist.[11] They are often understood in an essentialist way as mutually exclusive and, at best, as complementary: one is either a woman or a man, but not both or neither.[12] The words *man* and *woman* connote social agents, whereas *masculine* and *feminine* express cultural-religious ideals, values, and standards appropriate to one's gender. The cultural constructs of male and female and masculine and feminine constitute the Western sex/gender system that determines sex in terms of gender and constructs symbolic worlds in terms of gendered values. Gender, then, is not a biological or divinely sanctioned given but a sociopolitical construct and a principle of classification that generates psychological, social, cultural, religious, and political meanings and structures biological sexual identity.[13]

If one does not distinguish between sex as a biological given and gender as a cultural construct but sees both sex and gender as sociopolitical constructs, then the global sex/gender system appears

---

[11] For different cultural understandings of gender, see Serena Nanda, *Gender Diversity: Crosscultural Variations*, 2nd ed. (Long Grove, IL: Waveland Press, 2014).
[12] See Betsy Lucal, "What It Means to Be Gendered Me: Life on the Boundaries of a Dichotomous Gender System," *Gender and Society* 13, no. 6 (1999): 781–97.
[13] See, especially, Lorber, *Paradoxes of Gender*.

to be a commonsense cultural symbolic structure of representation. In short, as an ideological structure, gender actively naturalizes the sex/gender system through grammar, language, biology, and culture and makes its construction of sexual difference appear to be natural or G*d-given.

Language and Gender

Gendered language, in turn, reinscribes cultural-religious gender assumptions. Western androcentric languages and discourses do not just marginalize wo/men or eliminate them from historical records. Gendered language and grammar also express power relations and are, therefore, not just androcentric but also kyriocentric. Androcentric or kyriocentric languages construct the meaning of being a wo/man or a man not only differently but also in terms of unequal power relations.

Hence, not only feminist studies, in general, and religious studies, in particular, but also all intellectual work must confront the linguistic problem of the obfuscating function of gendered kyriocentric language. Grammatically, masculine language functions as so-called generic language, but this "conventional" language-function obscures wo/men. Wo/men are subsumed under masculine-typed language expressions such as citizens, presidents, and chairmen—"generic" terms that are not only masculine but also kyrios-determined language. In order to lift into consciousness the linguistic violence of so-called generic, masculine, male-centered language, I use the term *wo/men* and not *men* in an inclusive way. I suggest that whenever you read wo/men you understand it in the generic inclusive sense. In English, wo/men includes men, s/he includes he, and fe/male includes male. (However, this wordplay is only possible in English, not in Spanish or German, which makes such an inclusive/generic hearing/speaking very difficult.)

Feminist studies of language have elaborated that Western, androcentric grammatical systems understand language as both generic and gender specific. Wo/men must always think at least twice, if not three times, in order to adjudicate whether or not we are included in so-called generic terms such as "men," "humans," "Americans," "Christians," or "professors." However, we must not overlook that the meaning of the gender marker *woman* is unstable and shifting; it depends not so much on its sex/gender relation but on the sociopolitical context of the time and place in which it is used. For example, the word *woman* today is used interchangeably with *female* and thus has become a generic, sex/gender-based term, although until very recently it was applied to lower-class females only, whereas upper-class, refined females were "ladies." One can perceive the historical ambiguity of the term *woman* if one compares it with the term *lady*, an appellation that readily reveals its race, class, and colonial bias. Not only has *lady* been restricted to wo/men of higher status or educational refinement, but it has also symbolized *true womanhood* and *femininity*. A statement such as "slaves were not wo/men" offends our commonsense understanding, whereas a statement such as "slaves were not ladies" makes perfect sense.

The lady, slave mistress, or mother is the other of the lord, slave master, and father. All other wo/men are marked as inferior by race, class, religion, or culture, and function as the "others" of the "other" who are not mentioned at all. One can illustrate how such supposedly generic language works with reference to social position in advertisements that often read something like "University X is an affirmative-action institution and invites applications from African, Asian, Hispanic, or Native Americans and wo/men," as though these different types of Americans are all men, and wo/men do not belong to racial and ethnic minority groups. Men are not gendered but defined by their racial and cultural affiliation whereas wo/men are defined only by gender and seem not to belong to such racial and ethnic minority groups The word *wo/men*, therefore, has to be added to the ethnic-cultural definitions African, Asian, Hispanic, or Native American. Wo/men are thus doubly invisible in gendered language systems.

Sociopolitical classifications of gender, like grammatical ones, do not always correspond to a biological binary of sex. Anthropologists have pointed out that not all cultures and languages know of only two sexes/genders, and historians of gender have argued that even in Western culture the dual sex/gender system is of modern origin. Historian Thomas Laqueur, for instance, has maintained that a decisive shift took place in modernity from the ancient one-sex model to the present two-sex model.[14] Wo/men were once believed to have the same sex and genitals as men except that the wo/men's were inside the body as opposed to the men's, which were outside. In this one-sex model, the vagina was understood to be an interior penis; the labia, foreskin; the uterus, scrotum; and the ovaries, testicles. Gender, not biological sex, was the primary category determining the order of things.

What it meant to be a man or a woman in the ancient one-sex model was determined by one's social rank and place in the household, not by one's sexual organs. As a free man or a slave woman, one performed a cultural role according to one's social status and was not thought to be organically one of two incommensurable sexes. Not sex but the social status of the free, elite, propertied male head of household determined superior gender status. Hence, the ancients did not need to resort to sexual difference for supporting the claim that freeborn wo/men were inferior to freeborn men. Rather, because freeborn wo/men were subordinates, their "nature" was believed to be inferior.

During the Enlightenment in the eighteenth century, the two-sex model—the notion that there are two stable, opposite sexes—emerged. In this period originated the notion that the economic, political, and cultural lives of wo/men and men (their gender roles) are based on two biologically given sexes. Just as in antiquity the body was seen as reflecting the cosmological order, so in modernity the

---

[14] Thomas Laqueur, *Making Sex: Body and Gender from the Greeks to Freud* (Cambridge, MA: Harvard University Press, 1990).

body and sexuality are seen as representing and legitimating the sociopolitical order.

The social and political changes wrought by modernity produced the change from the one-sex to the asymmetrical two-sex model just as it engendered theories of racial inferiority. Because the Enlightenment's claims for democracy and equality excluded freeborn wo/men and subordinate men from full citizenship, new arguments had to be fashioned if elite freeborn men were to justify elite wo/men's exclusion from the public domain. The promise of democracy, that wo/men and disenfranchised men were full citizens, generated new antifeminist, sexist, and racist arguments based on nature, physiology, and science. Those who opposed, for instance, the democratic participation of freeborn wo/men sought evidence for wo/men's mental and physical unsuitability for the public sphere by arguing that wo/men's bodies and biology made them unfit to participate. Similar arguments were made with respect to subordinate men and colonialized peoples.

The theory of "separate spheres" for men and wo/men thus arose alongside the dual-sex/gender model. In Enlightenment discourses, elite wo/men were no longer construed as lesser men but as totally different from and complementary to men, as beings of a "purer race" or an "angelic species" less affected than men by sexual drives and desires. In order to bar wo/men from participation in the new civil society, the physical and moral differences between men and wo/men were conceived to ensure that elite wo/men and subordinate people were excluded from political decision making. Two incommensurable sexes/genders were the result of these ideological practices. However, one must not overlook that these gendered identity constructs primarily applied to elite bourgeois wo/men.

Contemporary feminist work on gender has attempted to unravel the politics of the modern sex/gender system as the product of various social technologies, institutional discourses, and practices of daily life. Gender as a sociocultural construct does not connote a biological, anthropological, or psychological given but is a semiotic marker that assigns meaning to individuals within a society. Individuals recognize gender and "appropriate" gender ascriptions because they perceive them as real. Gender is thus a product and process of not only representation but also self-identity. The recognition of wo/men's own participation in the construction of gender makes it possible to see that gender can also be deconstructed or differently constructed. Understanding gender as a product and process makes it possible for feminist theory to analyze cultural masculinity and femininity with the intention of changing them.

Generally, accepted gender expectations define the socially recognized genders in a given society. The gendered division of labor assigns work according to gender, whereas kinship spells out family rights and responsibilities for each gender. Gender scripts prescribe and proscribe behavior and grant prerogatives. Social controls, which reward conforming behavior and stigmatize aberrant conduct, produce personalities that perform cultural gender dictates. Finally, law, custom, and religion reinforce gender ideology and imagery, or the cultural representations of gender in symbolic language and artistic production, in ways that legitimate and support dominant gender statuses.

For instance, the modern ethos of femininity prescribes that "good" wo/men perform unpaid services inside and outside the family and inculcates the so-called feminine virtues of selfless love, nurturing care, and loving-kindness. "True womanhood" defines woman's nature as "being for others" in actual or spiritual motherhood. Whereas men are measured by the masculine standards of self-assertion, independence, power, and control, wo/men are called to fulfill their true nature and destiny in self-sacrificing, loving care, and motherhood. Moreover, Christian teachings of self-sacrificing love and humble service reinforce and perpetuate this cultural socialization of wo/men to selfless femininity and altruistic self-negation.

In antiquity, for instance, menial service was seen as appropriate to the nature of slaves and serfs of either sex/gender; in modern times, it is construed as a feminine ideal appropriate to the nature of wo/men. Public political service in turn is conceptualized as masculine and appropriate to the nature of men. This separation between the public male sphere and the private female domain has been at the root of an economic system that frequently leaves female-headed households destitute, a development that has particularly devastating effects on wo/men and children in both developing and industrialized countries.

Although maleness and femaleness are supposedly biological givens, they are actually cultural norms backed by social sanctions and enforced by medical procedures.[15] Gender as an individual identity structure rests on the ascription of a certain sex from birth or even before. Gender identity constitutes a sense of self, and it determines marital and procreative status as well as sexual orientation that patterns sexual desires, feelings, and identifications. The so-called normal outcome is the heterosexually gendered personality fashioned by socially normative patterns and emotions inculcated through family structure, parenting, and education.

Finally, gendered practices internalize learned social gender behavior, sexual cues, and gender socialization and interaction, while gender display presents the self as a masculine or feminine person through dress, cosmetics, weight control, and other bodily regimes. Thus, wo/men's "second-class" status is achieved not by force but rather in and through socialization and cultural practices of femininity. Religion has played a major role in the construction and symbolic legitimization of such naturalized gender relations.

Religion and Gender[16]

Feminist the*logies and gender studies in religion have sought to bring about a paradigm shift in the way religion and religious texts,

---

[15] See Anne Fausto-Sterling, *Sexing the Body: Gender Politics and the Construction of Sexuality* (New York: Basic Books, 2000). For an attempt at wrestling with the issue of intersex from a Christian the*logical perspective, see Megan K. DeFranza, *Sex Difference in Christian Theology: Male, Female, and Intersex in the Image of God* (Grand Rapids, MI: Eerdmans, 2015), esp. 23–67, for a comprehensive review of the literature.

[16] See especially the excellent work of Mireya Baltodano, Gabriela Miranda García, and Elisabeth Cook, eds., *Género y Religión* (San José, Costa Rica: Universidad Bíblica Latinoamericana, 2009). See Durre S. Ahmed, ed., *Gendering the Spirit: Women, Religion, and the Postcolonial Response* (New York: Palgrave, 2002); Elizabeth A. Castelli, ed., *Women, Gender, and Religion: A Reader* (New York: Palgrave, 2001); Rebecca S. Chopp, *The Power to Speak: Feminism, Language, and God* (New York: Crossroad, 1989); and Juschka, *Feminism in the Study of Religion.*

traditions, and communities have been seen and studied. They have sought to change and transform the tradition by engaging in a wide-ranging critique of disciplinary presuppositions, methods, and epistemology as well as through creative reimagination and transformation of religious discourses and institutions. They have thereby sought to rediscover and elaborate wo/men's subjectivity and agency within religious histories and contemporary communities. Insofar as feminist theory has revealed the gender encoding of all knowledge, feminist studies in religion have been able to show the gendering of religious knowledge and religious institutions. Feminist scholars in religion have also used gender theories to understand the second-class status of wo/men in religion.[17]

In many religions, men and masculinity are associated with the divine and the transcendent, whereas wo/men and femininity are seen as immanent, impure, profane, evil, and sinful. Many religious traditions—Judaism, Christianity, Islam, Hinduism, Taoism, and Buddhism—use binary gender oppositions to construct their kyriarchal symbolic universes.[18] The deity (Jahwe, Allah, or Christ) is understood as not only masculine but also all-powerful ruler and judge, whereas wo/men are associated with sin, death, and sex (Eve, Lilith, or Kali). Men have been, and still are, representatives of the divine and religious leaders in the major religions of the world. Wo/men in turn have been excluded from religious leadership, official teaching, and sacred ritual.

Because religious symbolic systems are heavily gendered in masculine terms, they reinforce cultural gender roles and concepts and

---

[17] I have been puzzled by the enthusiastic reception of gender analysis by feminist theologians in Latin America at a time when a critique of gender analysis in favor of intersectional analysis emerged in the United States. However, this phenomenon becomes understandable if one takes into account that the intellectual frame of gender analysis in Latin America was liberation the*logy, which eschewed gender analysis, whereas that of feminist the*logy in the United States and Europe was women's and gender studies.

[18] See, for example, Juschka, *Feminism in the Study of Religion*; Zilka Spahic-Siljak, ed., *Contesting Female, Feminist and Muslim Identities: Post-Socialist Contexts of Bosnia and Herzegovina and Kosovo* (Sarajevo: Center for Interdisciplinary Postgraduate Studies, 2012); Tamar Ross, *Expanding the Palace of Torah: Orthodoxy and Feminism* (Lebanon, NH: University Press of New England, 2004); Namsoon Kang, *Diasporic Feminist Theology: Asia and the Theopolitical Imagination* (Minneapolis, MN: Fortress, 2014); and Aquino and Rosado-Nunes, *Feminist Intercultural Theology*.

legitimize them as ordained by G*d or as the "order of creation." For instance, as feminist scholar Judith Plaskow has argued, Christian male the*logians have formulated the*logical concepts in terms of their own cultural experience, insisting on male language relating to G*d and on a symbolic universe in which wo/men do not appear.[19] Similar observations can be made regarding other world religions.

Since the Industrial Revolution in Europe and America at the beginning of the nineteenth century, religion has been pushed out of the public realm and relegated to the private sphere of individualistic piety, charitable work, and the cultivation of home and family. Religion has become culturally feminized while its leadership has remained predominantly male. Nevertheless, both religion and wo/men were crucial in shaping Western identity. For instance, as a "missionary religion," Christianity had the same function as the Euro-American, refined upper-class "White Lady": to "civilize the savages" who were understood as having an "untamed nature."

Today, the Vatican is actively involved in reshaping the United Nations' stress on gender equality and gender justice in terms of the "dignity of woman" ideology, which insists on the difference and complementarity of woman to man.[20] These ecclesiastical pronouncements recognize the notion of gender but define it in terms of heterosexuality and biological gender or sex.[21] However, such an essentialist and biological definition of gender as the "feminine genius" overlooks that wo/men are not only gendered but also defined by race, class, and imperialist structures. In medieval times,

---

[19] Judith Plaskow. *Sex, Sin, and Grace: Women's Experience and the Theologies of Niebuhr and Tillich* (Washington, DC: University Press of America, 1980). See also Judith Plaskow, *Standing at Sinai Again: Judaism from a Feminist Perspective* (New York: HarperCollins, 1991).

[20] See Joanne Omang, "Playing Hardball against Women's Rights: The Holy See at the UN," *Conscience* 34, no. 2, November 2, 2013, http://churchandstate.org.uk/2013/08/playing-hardball-against-womens-rights-the-holy-see-at-the-un/.

[21] See Jadranka Rebeka Anic's excellent article "Gender Politik und die Katholische Kirche," in *Feminist Theology in Europe: A Reader in Honor of Hedwig Meyer-Wilmes*, eds. Elzbieta Adamiak and Marie Theres Wacker (Münster: LIT Verlag, 2013), 64–79, esp. 70.

Roman Catholic the*logians subscribed to the Aristotelian model of wo/man's inferiority and subordination, and in the nineteenth and twentieth centuries advocated an essentialist Romantic gender definition in terms of the White Lady in order to exclude middle- and upper-class white wo/men from both religious ordination and participation in the workforce. Today its the*logizing of the "feminine genius" is still directed against wo/men in ordained office as well as wo/men's sexual-bodily self-determination through birth control and the right to end pregnancy.

In short, I understand gender as a sociopolitical institution as well as an ideological representation. The assumption of natural sex/gender differences serves as a preconstructed framework for individuals and cultural institutions. Moreover, by presenting the dualistic sex/gender system of male and female or masculine and feminine as universal and essential, this frame of meaning obscures the reality that the very notion of two genders/sexes is a sociopolitical construct for maintaining domination and not a biological given or ideological essence. Not all cultures know only two sexes or use gendered languages.[22] Sexual differences depend on sociocultural communicative practices and, therefore, can be developed differently or changed. Such a focus on "woman and the feminine," consciously or not, works with an essentialist notion of "woman" that is culturally elaborated in the Barbie-doll image of the White Lady. This image of the ideal wo/man is propagated by the media not only in Western countries, but also around the globe. Yet, gender is always already differently inflected by race, class, age, sexuality, imperialism, and other power structures. If that is the case, one must refuse to develop a feminist analytic in terms of the essentialist dualistic category "woman" as the other.

Political philosophy continues to assume that the propertied, educated, elite Western man is defined by reason, self-determination,

---

[22] Satoko Yamaguchi addresses the problem of biblical translation from a gendered into to a status language in "Father Image of God and Inclusive Language: A Reflection in Japan," in *Toward a New Heaven and Earth: Essays in Honor of Elisabeth Schüssler Fiorenza*, ed. Fernando Segovia (Maryknoll, NY: Orbis, 2003), 198–224.

and full citizenship, whereas wo/men and other subordinated peoples are defined by emotion, service, and dependence. Wo/men are seen not as rational and responsible adults but as emotional and helpless children, "beasts of burden," or sex objects. Perhaps it goes without saying that white, Euro-American, elite, educated men have articulated such modern (and postmodern) understandings of rationality and the world, prejudices that have been supported by Christian the*logical and other religious traditions and have in turn determined modern, neoliberal kyriarchal forms and ideologies of democracy. These men have not only defined white wo/men as others but have also regarded all others of the *others* as "second-class citizens" lacking basic human qualities.

In her blog "What Is Otherness?" Zuleyka Zevallos distinguishes between psychological and sociological approaches to identity construction. She explains:

> The idea of *"otherness"* is central to sociological analyses of how majority and minority identities are constructed. This is because the representation of different groups within any given society is controlled by groups that have greater political power. In order to understand the notion of the Other, sociologists first seek to put a critical spotlight on the ways in which social identities are constructed. Identities are often thought as being natural or innate—something that we are born with—but sociologists highlight that this taken-for-granted view is not true.[23]

I would argue that the Other is not one identity but consists of many different others whose identities are sociopolitically constructed.[24] We

---

[23] Zuleyka Zevallos, "What Is Otherness?" *Other Sociologist*, June 6, 2015, http://othersociologist.com/otherness-resources/.

[24] According to Wikipedia, "The *Other* or *constitutive Other* (also the verb forms *othering* or *otherize*) is a key concept in continental philosophy and the social sciences; it opposes the *Same*. The Other and 'Otherness' refers to that which is alien and divergent from that which is given, such as a norm, identity, or the self. The Constitutive Other often denotes a different, incomprehensible self outside of one's own; thus the spelling is often capitalized, because the Other is a mystification fetishized by a hegemonic subject" ("Other" *Wikipedia*, http://en.wikipedia.org/wiki/Other, accessed September 22, 2015).

need an analytic tool to better understand such sociopolitical constructions. Hence, I have argued, the key analytic concepts for feminist
analysis are not woman, patriarchy, the feminine, or gender. Rather,
the feminist task is to analyze systems of domination, which I have
named *kyriarchy* and of which gender is only one structure, albeit an
important one. Such interlocking structures of domination create and
determine not just one but many others.

While, in my understanding, feminist the*logy engages both
wo/men and gender studies for its work, it is not identical with and
cannot be limited to them. Rather, both feminist political theory and
the*logy focus on issues of power and structures of domination in
light of wo/men's struggles against kyriarchal relations. Thus, I understand feminist the*logy and studies in religion as social-cultural-polit-
ical studies of domination and struggle that need to explore how
solidarity is possible and shaped in the context of these structures.

A critical feminist theory articulates the subject of feminist struggles not on the basis of the essential difference of wo/men or of sociocultural gender differences but rather in the interest of naming
feminist subjects who struggle against structures of domination.[25]
Wo/men are not just gendered but also determined by race, heteronormativity, class, and colonialism.[26] Like gender, the social relations
that give rise to theories of race, class, or ethnic differences are also
socioculturally constructed as relations of domination and not simply
biological givens. Nineteenth-century scientists constructed the so-
called lower races—lower-class wo/men, sexual deviants, criminals,
urban poor, and the insane—as biological "races apart." Their differences from the white male and their likenesses to each other
"explained" their lower position in the social kyriarchy.

In this scheme, the lower races represent the "feminine" aspect of
the human species, and wo/men represent the "lower race" of gender.

---

25 See Jutta Sommerbauer, *Differenzen zwischen Frauen: Zur Positionsbestimmung und
Kritik des Postmodernen Feminismus* (Münster: Unrast Verlag, 2003).
26 Eske Wollrad, *Weisssein im Widerspruch: Feministische Perspektiven auf Rassismus*, Kultur und Religion (Königstein/Taunus: Helmer Verlag, 2005).

Thus, wo/men do not share a unitary essence but are multiple and fractured in many different ways by race, class, age, sexuality, ability, and gender. To indicate this fracturedness linguistically, I have introduced the writing of *wo/men* with a slash. In addition to highlighting the obfuscation of wo/men in androcentric language systems, this mode of writing *wo/men* seeks to signify an intersectional definition of the feminist subject.

The*logically speaking, replacing the existing religious dual-sex model with that of the divine image that is neither male nor female, white nor black, rich nor poor, but multicolored and multigendered would open up the possibility of moving beyond the masculine monism of the one-sex model and the asymmetric dualism of the sex/gender system to an intersectional analysis of kyriarchal power. Such a process offers the prospect of deconstructing gender and fashioning identity and community in the variegated image of the divine in our midst.

Intersectional Kyriarchy[27]

Legal scholar Kimberlé Crenshaw coined the term *intersectionality*, which entails "the notion that subjectivity is constituted by mutually multiplicative vectors of race, gender, class, sexuality, and imperialism."[28] Crenshaw was responding to the tendency within identity politics to overlook or silence intragroup differences to the detriment of black wo/men. She pointed to the simultaneous race and gender dimensions of violence against wo/men by looking at responses to domestic violence and rape in order to draw attention to

---

[27] For further explication, see Elisabeth Schüssler Fiorenza, *The Power of the Word: Scripture and the Rhetoric of Empire* (Minneapolis, MN: Fortress, 2007), and Elisabeth Schüssler Fiorenza, *Democratizing Biblical Studies: Toward an Emancipatory Educational Space* (Louisville, KY: Westminster John Knox, 2009).

[28] Kimberlé Williams Crenshaw, "Mapping the Margins: Intersectionality, Identity Politics, and Violence against Women of Color," in *The Feminist Philosophy Reader*, eds. Alison Bailey and Chris Cuomo (New York: McGraw-Hill, 2008), 279–309. See also Jennifer C. Nash, "Rethinking Intersectionality," *Feminist Review* 89, no. 1 (2008): 1–15, esp. 3.

the ways in which the specificity of black wo/men's experiences of violence is ignored, overlooked, misrepresented, and/or silenced. Crenshaw focuses on both the structural and political aspects of the intersectionality of violence against wo/men of color in order to highlight the importance of intersectionality and of engaging an intersectional lens.

The theory of intersectionality has been articulated threefold: as a theory of marginalized subjectivity, as a theory of identity, and as a theory of the matrix of oppressions. In the first iteration, intersectional theory refers only to multiply marginalized subjects. In its second iteration, the theory seeks to illuminate how identity is constructed at the intersections of race, gender, class, sexuality, and imperialism. The third iteration stresses intersectional theory as a theory of structures and sites of oppression. Race, sex, gender, class, and imperialism are seen as vectors of dominating power that create co-constitutive social processes that engender the differential simultaneity of dominations and subordinations.

Since wo/men's and gender studies have tended to focus on male/masculine power over wo/men and feminine gender ideology but not on race, class, heteronormativity, colonialism, and other power structures of domination, a new mode of analysis became necessary. If race, class, and colonialism come into view, then the gender dualism of masculine-feminine is transposed into the dualisms "first-world/two-thirds-world wo/men" or "white wo/men and wo/men of color."[29]

Intersectional analysis thus destabilizes the dualistic gender-identity framework that engenders the dichotomy between the space marked "white wo/men/first-world wo/men" and the space marked "wo/men of color/two-thirds-world wo/men." Identity politics claims that white, first-world feminists can speak only about and in the name

---

[29] In order to highlight that the so-called third world constitutes the vast majority of people on the planet, the term *two-thirds world* has been coined to draw attention to the shocking inequality of wealth and resources around the neoliberal globe.

of white, first-world wo/men whereas wo/men of color/two-thirds-world wo/men are called to form coalitions and considered able to speak for all wo/men of the so-called two-thirds world. Feminist scholars in religion or the*logians, so this argument goes, cannot but articulate either a "white/first-world" or a "wo/men of color/two-thirds-world" the*logy and hermeneutics.

Over and against such a discursive either/or essentialist identity politics conceptualized in terms of gender, it needs to be pointed out that identity is constituted by not only gender but also race, immigrant status, class, education, nationality, sexuality, disability, religion, and many other distinctions. Hence, identity must be seen as multiplex and shaped by intersecting structures of dominations. One cannot assume that wo/men's identity is the same whether it is that of "wo/men of color" or that of "white wo/men."

At a 1989 workshop at Memphis State University on Integrating Race and Gender into the College Curriculum, sociologist and black feminist Patricia Hill Collins "introduced the basic idea of intersectionality as a paradigm for conceptualizing social reality" and argued that "we must first recognize race, class, and gender as *interlocking* categories of analysis that are inclusive of race, class, and gender as distinctive but interlocking structures of oppression." Instead of arguing "I am more oppressed than you," she suggests that wo/men "examine our different experiences within the more fundamental relationship of domination and subordination." Since a "piece of the oppressor" is "planted deep within each of us," we not only need to deploy race, class, and gender "as interlocking categories of analysis that cultivate profound differences in our personal biographies" but also to "transcend those very differences by reconceptualizing race, class, and gender to create new categories of connection."[30]

In light of Collins's analysis, I have argued that if wo/men are not just determined by gender but also by race, class, heteronormativity,

---

[30] Patricia Hill Collins, *On Intellectual Activism* (Philadelphia: Temple University Press, 2013), quotations on 213–15, emphasis added.

imperialism, and other such structures of domination, then it is necessary to develop a critical analytic that can deconstruct the global cultural kyriarchal gender paradigm of the White Lady and the power structures she embodies. However, we must be careful to conceptualize her "whiteness and femininity" not in essentialist-ontological but rather in historical-rhetorical terms. Hence, it is important to see gender as one among several structures of domination constructed to serve the division of power and wealth by sex, economics, race, culture, nationality, and religion.

Thus, feminist theory and practice must destabilize not only the essentialist markers of *woman* and *gender* but also those of heteronormativity, race, class, colonialism, age, disability, and so on. Feminists must concern themselves with both the patriarchal and kyriarchal power relations inscribed in sacred scriptures and religious traditions. A dualistic gender analysis does not suffice in biblical and religious studies because gender has been constructed in antiquity as kyriarchal in terms of the status of the freeborn lord (*kyrios*) or lady (*kyria*), and in modern times in terms of class, colonial, and race status.[31] As a consequence, intersectional analysis becomes necessary.

In short, it is crucial to recognize that gender as a sociopolitical and psychological practice of superiority and inferiority is only one of several social ascriptions that define the identity of and promote the exploitation of wo/men. If one realizes that gender intersects with race, class, age, religion, sexual preference, and ethnicity, then one can demystify binary gender oppositions. Conceptualizing gender as a practice that produces sex differences inflected by other categories allows one to see that individual wo/men are not simply gendered. Rather, the intersection of race, class, sexuality, nation, and religion construct what it means to be a "wo/man" differently in different sociopolitical and cultural contexts.

---

[31] For this concept, see María Lugones, "Heterosexualism and the Colonial Modern Gender System," *Hypatia* 22, no. 1 (2007) 186–209, and Maria Lugones, "Toward a Decolonial Feminism," *Hypatia* 25, no. 4 (2010): 742–59. See also Reina Lewis and Sara Mills, eds., *Feminist Postcolonial Theory: A Reader* (New York: Routledge, 2003).

Variegated feminist, postcolonial, and critical race theories have come together in developing the analytic of intersectionality as an instrument to analyze the complex situation of global domination and to demonstrate that the structures of heteronormativity, gender, race, and class are inextricably intertwined.[32] However, these structures are often seen as working alongside each other but have not been theoretically integrated to perform a critical intersectional kyriarchal analysis.

In order to bring these various theoretical perspectives together, I coined the neologism *kyriarchy* as a replacement of the key feminist analytic concept of *patriarchy*[33] in order to highlight that the analytic object of feminist theory and the*logy is not simply woman or gender but the intersectionality of domination, or kyriarchy.[34] Kyriarchy, understood as a gradated system of dominations, is derived, on the one hand, from the Greek word *kyrios* (Latin *dominus*)—the lord, slave master, father, husband, and/or propertied freeborn male to whom all the members of the household were subordinated and by whom they were controlled—and, on the other hand, the verb *archein*—to rule, dominate, or control. In Greco-Roman antiquity, the sociopolitical system of kyriarchy was institutionalized either as empire or as a democratic political form of ruling that excluded all freeborn and slave wo/men from full citizenship and decision-making powers.[35]

---

[32] Lyn Weber, *Understanding Race, Class, Gender, and Sexuality. A Conceptual Framework*, 2nd ed. (New York: Oxford University Press, 2010). See also Helma Lutz, Maria Theresa Herrera Vivar, and Linda Supik, eds., *Focus Intersektionalität. Bewegungen und Verortungen eines vielschichtigen Konzepts* (Wiesbaden: VS Verlag, 2010); and Nina Lykke, *Feminist Studies: A Guide to Intersectional Theory, Methodology, and Writing* (New York: Routledge, 2010).

[33] See Valerie Bryson, ed., *Feminist Political Theory: An Introduction*, 2nd ed. (New York: Palgrave, 2003), 163–225.

[34] Gabriele Winker and Nina Degele, *Intersektionalität. Zur Analyse sozialer Ungleichheiten* (Bielefeld, transcript Verlag, 2009); Lutz, Herrera Vivar, and Supik, eds., *Focus Intersektionalität*; and Sharon Doetsch-Kidder, *Social Change and Intersectional Activism: The Spirit of Social Movement: The Politics of Intersectionality* (New York: Palgrave, 2012).

[35] For a fuller discussion, see the path-breaking book by Susan Moller Okin, *Women in Western Political Thought* (Princeton, NJ: Princeton University Press, 1979), with an extensive afterword in the 1992 2nd ed., 308–86. See also Schüssler Fiorenza, *In Memory of Her*.

Furthermore, kyriarchy functions as a sociopolitical and cultural-religious system of domination that structures the identity slots open to members of society in terms of race, gender, nation, age, economy, and sexuality. These identity slots or categories are configured in terms of pyramidal relations of domination and submission, profit, and exploitation. Kyriarchy is best theorized as a complex pyramidal system of intersecting multiplicative social and religious relations of superordination and subordination, of ruling and exploitation. Kyriarchal relations of domination are built on elite male property rights as well as on the exploitation, dependency, inferiority, and obedience of wo/men, who are understood to signify all those subordinated. Such kyriarchal relations of domination are characteristic of the Roman Empire and are still at work today in the multiplicative intersectional structures of discrimination.

Hence, a critical intersectional feminist analytic does not understand domination as an essentialist, ahistorical dualistic system. Instead, it articulates it as kyriarchy, as a *heuristic* (derived from the Greek, meaning "to find") concept, or as a diagnostic, analytic instrument that enables investigation into the multiplicative interaction of gender, race, class, and imperial stratifications and asks for research into their discursive inscriptions and ideological reproductions. Moreover, it highlights that people inhabit several shifting structural positions at the same time. If one subject position of domination becomes privileged, it constitutes a nodal point. While in any particular historical moment, class or imperialism may be the primary modality through which one experiences class, imperialism, gender, and race, in other circumstances, gender may be the privileged position through which one experiences those other categories.

The Western kyriarchal system works simultaneously on four interrelated levels, each of which strengthens the other's dominating power: sociopolitical, ethical-cultural, biological-natural, and linguistic-symbolic. Womanist, queer, Latina, and other postcolonial feminist the*logies work on different nodal sites of the intersecting discourse levels of kyriarchy and hence emphasize different aspects of the kyriarchal system. Kyriarchal power is both repressive and productive. While I agree with Michel Foucault's argument that democratic power is not concentrated in the person of the sovereign, such power still needs to be spelled out in political terms.[36] Sociopolitical analysis of intersectional kyriarchy thus calls for a sociopolitical delineation.

Yet, as I noted in the introduction, intersectional theorists usually conceptualize such social and ideological structures of domination as *hierarchical* in order to map and make visible the complex interstructuring of the conflicting status positions of different wo/men and understand neoliberal gender exploitation as hierarchically structured. However, such a labeling of neoglobal structures of domination as "hierarchical" or "holy" and sacrosanct ascribes them to G*d or religion rather than to the agents of domination. Merriam-Webster defines *hierarchy* as

1:    a division of angels
2a: a ruling body of clergy organized into orders or ranks, each subordinate to the one above it; especially the bishops of a province or nation
2b: church government by a hierarchy
3:    a body of persons in authority
4:    the classification of a group of people according to ability or to economic, social, or professional standing; *also*: the group so classified
5:    a graded or ranked series; a *hierarchy* of values[37]

Hence, the label "hierarchical" for such a pyramidal system of domination is clearly a misnomer, since it only targets one specific

---

[36] "According to (Michel) Foucault, power subjects individuals in both senses of the term: Individuals are both subject to the constraints of social relations of power and simultaneously enabled to take up the position of a *subject* in and through those very constraints . . . a uniquely modern modality of power, one that differs from previous modalities, that it is capillary, local and spread throughout the social body, rather than concentrated in the center of the state in the person of the sovereign" (Amy Allen, *The Power of Feminist Theory: Domination, Resistance, Solidarity* [Boulder: University of Colorado Press, 1999], 33).

[37] See "Hierarchy," *Merriam-Webster*, http://www.merriam-webster.com/dictionary/hierarchy.

form of "power over"—power that is religiously sanctioned as sacred—derived from Greek: *hieros* (sacred/holy) and *archein* (rule/dominate). To lift this misnomer into consciousness, I have proposed that we replace the categories of patriarchy and hierarchy with kyriarchy.[38] I suggest that an analytic of domination needs to adopt a critical intersectional analysis to name global neoliberalism as domination, as kyriarchy.[39] Contemporary gender and other power relations are not religiously (in other words, hierarchically) structured—that is, they are not defined by holy, religious power relations. Rather, they are structured primarily by sociopolitical, economic, and cultural systems of domination, such as racism, heterosexism, classism, or imperialism. They are structured by neoliberalist kyriarchy.

Global neoliberal kyriarchy is best theorized as intersecting multiplicative social, economic, and religious structures of superordination and subordination, domination and exploitation, and ruling and oppression. Kyriarchal relations of domination are built on elite male property rights and privileges as well as on wo/men's exploitation, dependency, inferiority, and obedience. Such kyriarchal relations are still at work today in the multiplicative intersections of class, race, gender, ethnicity, empire, and other structures of discrimination in our lives.

---

[38] For a fuller elaboration of kyriarchy/kyriocentrism, see Elisabeth Schüssler Fiorenza, "Toward an Intersectional Analytic: Race, Gender, Ethnicity, and Empire in Early Christian Studies," in *Prejudice and Christian Beginnings*, eds. Laura Nasrallah and Elisabeth Schüssler Fiorenza (Minneapolis, MN: Fortress, 2009).

[39] For the first development of this analytic, see Schüssler Fiorenza, *But She Said*, 103–32, and Elisabeth Schüssler Fiorenza, "Religion, Gender, and Society: Shaping the Discipline of Religious/Theological Studies," in *The Relevance of Theology*, eds. Carl Reinhold Bråckenhielm and Gunhild Winqvist Hollman (Uppsala, Sweden: Uppsala Universitet, 2002), 85–99. While the notion of kyriarchy has not been widely discussed in feminist theoretical works, it has engendered a wide-ranging discussion among young feminists on the Internet. See, for example, "Accepting Kyriarchy, Not Apologies," My Ecdysis: A Radical Preference for Love (blog), April 26, 2008, http://myecdysis.blogspot.com/2008/04/accepting-kyriarchy-not-apologies.html; and Rachel McCarthy James, "Why I Use That Word That I Use: Cis, Cissupremacy, Cissexism," Deeply Problematic (blog), August 18, 2010, http://www.deeply problematic.com/2010/08/why-i-use-that-word-that-i-use-cis.html.

In the last 300 years or more, the struggles of wo/men, black people, workers, and poor and immigrant peoples (to mention a few) have argued for full citizen rights These struggles are not struggles of the past, but are still ongoing today in the struggles against neoliberal globalization.[40] For instance, in the fourth century BCE, Aristotle argued that the freeborn, propertied, educated Greek man was the highest of moral beings and that all other members of the human race were defined by their functions in his service. Even today's neoliberal kyriarchal societies need a "servant class" or people, be they slaves, serfs, house servants, kulaks, or migrant workers. The existence of a gendered "servant class" is maintained through law, education, social-ization, and brute violence. This is sustained by the belief that mem-bers of a "servant class" are inferior by nature or by divine decree to those whom they are destined to serve.

As we have seen in the introduction, today's context of such dis-criminatory politics is the "new world order" of neoliberalism span-ning the globe. Neoliberalism preaches "the clash of civilizations" and seeks to maximize financial returns and profits as much as possi-ble for the world's richest 1 percent. The predictable results of the neoliberal economic model are socially unjust, politically destabiliz-ing, culturally destructive, and ecologically unsustainable. Economic globalization has been created with the specific goals of giving pri-macy to corporate profits and installing and codifying such market values globally. Furthermore, economic globalization amalgamates and merges all economic activities around the world within a single model of global monoculture.[41]

Since nation-states seem no longer to be in control of globaliza-tion, social and political theorists have argued that globalization

---

[40] See Christa Wichterich, *The Globalized Woman: Reports from a Future of Inequality* (New York: Zed, 2000); Ann-Cathrin Jarl, *In Justice: Women and Global Economics* (Minneapolis, MN: Fortress, 2003); Marjori Agosín, *Women, Gender, and Human Rights: A Global Perspective* (New Brunswick, NJ: Rutgers University Press, 2001); and Beverly Wildung Harrison, *Justice in the Making: Feminist Social Ethics* (Louisville, KY: Westminster John Knox, 2004).

[41] See Harvey, *Brief History of Neoliberalism.*

threatens democracy and human rights. As essayist and novelist Arundhati Roy points out:

> The [neoliberal capitalists] have mastered the technique of infiltrating the instruments of democracy—the "independent" judiciary, the "free" press, the parliament—and molding them to their purpose. The project of corporate globalization has cracked the core: Free elections, a free press, and an independent judiciary mean little when the free market has reduced them to commodities available to the highest bidder.[42]

Insofar as multinational corporations have taken over many of the functions of the nation-state, their globalizing economic, cultural, and political forces form a polycentric kyriarchy. The danger of this shift from nation-state to international corporation is that lobbyists of transnational corporations manipulate democratic governments, and the system of global capitalism can no longer be held democratically accountable.

We must not overlook, however, that the economic-ecological impact of globalization, and its attendant exploitation and misery, has also engendered the resurgence of the Religious Right and of global cultural and religious fundamentalisms claiming the power to define the true nature and essence of religion. Right-wing, well-financed religious think tanks are supported by reactionary political and financial institutions that seek to defend kyriarchal capitalism. In the past decades, right-wing religious movements around the globe have insisted either on the figuration of emancipated wo/men as signifiers of Western decadence and of modern atheistic secularism or the presentation of masculinist power as the expression of divine power. The interconnection between religious antidemocratic arguments and the debate regarding wo/men's place and role is not accidental or of merely intrareligious significance.

---

[42] Arundhati Roy, *An Ordinary Person's Guide to Empire* (Cambridge, MA: South End, 2004), 3. Please note, this statement was articulated before corporations were recognized as citizens by the US Supreme Court.

In short, rather than identifying kyriarchal domination in dualistic terms with the binaries of male over female, white over black, Western over-colonized peoples, it is best to understand it as an intersectional pyramidal system shaped by race, gender, class, colonial, or imperial dominations. Development sociologist Shelley Feldman's work helps highlight the ways in which kyriarchy connotes "the multiple relations of ruling that include the way in which gender relations articulate with economies, states, and markets," and, I would add, religions. Such an analysis "can explore relations of domination as mediating processes of negotiation constituted by complex identities and practices rather than by an assumed universalized unitary, dominating force of male (white, colonial, elite, imperial) domination and female (black, colonialized, underdog) subordination."[43]

In short, kyriarchal democracies are stratified by such shifting intersections that shape the *structural positions* that are assigned to us more or less by birth. However, how people live these positions is conditioned not simply by the structures themselves, but also by the *subject positions* through which we live them. Whereas an essentialist approach assigns to people an "authentic" identity that is derived from our structural position, one's subject position becomes coherent and compelling through political discourse, interpretive frameworks, and the development of theoretical horizons regarding domination. For Christians, biblical religion plays a key role in shaping such subject positions.

Kyriarchal Religion and Neoliberal Globalization

Feminist scholars in religion insist that religious texts and traditions must be reinterpreted so that wo/men and other "nonpersons" can achieve full citizenship in religion and society, gain full access to decision-making powers, and learn how to live out radical equality in religious communities. We argue that differences of sex/gender, race,

---

[43] Shelley Feldman, "Exploring Theories of Patriarchy: A Perspective from Contemporary Bangladesh," *Signs* 26, no. 4 (2001): 1097–1127, esp. 1101.

class, and ethnicity are socioculturally constructed and not willed by G*d and, therefore, must be changed. G*d, who created people in the divine image, has called every individual differently and is to be found in and among people who are created equal.

In *The Handmaid's Tale*, Canadian author Margaret Atwood presented a political novel that displays the discursive practices of the kyriarchal politics of othering and subordination inscribed in sacred scriptures. Atwood's narrative articulates the interstructuring of prejudices: sexism, racism, and class differences, on the one hand, and the availability of the Bible as language and legitimization for totalitarian ends, on the other. *The Handmaid's Tale* describes a future totalitarian society whose structures and language are modeled after the Bible. While the novel is written in light of Christian scriptures, the kyriarchal biblical frame of prejudice it exposes is not solely engraved in Christian scriptures.

The novel's narrator and protagonist is a woman whose real name and identity the reader never learns. She is a handmaid called "Offred" who lives in the Republic of Gilead, which has replaced the United States of America and is ruled by a group espousing an ideology similar to that of the Moral Majority in the pre-Gileadean society of the late twentieth century. After the president and congress of the United States have been massacred, the modern biblical republic is established. Wo/men lose their right to property and employment, and the black population (referred to as the children of Ham) are resettled in segregated "National Homelands." Furthermore, Jews are repatriated through what are called "boat-person plans." In this biblical republic, reading and writing are outlawed, the news media is censored and controlled, and everyone is required to spy on everyone. Because the Bible is the foundational document for the Republic of Gilead, it is reserved for the elite and only to be read by men in power:

> The Bible is kept locked up, the way people once kept tea locked up, so the servants wouldn't steal it. It is an incendiary device: who knows what we'd make of it, if we ever got our hands on it? We can be read

to from it, by him, but we cannot read. Our heads turn towards him, we are expectant, here comes our bedtime story. . . . He has something we don't have, he has the word. How we squandered it, once.[44]

Atwood's narrator not only discloses the dehumanizing horrors of the totalitarian kyriarchal state but also the belief of those in power that the Bible could be an "incendiary device" in the hands of "the subordinate others," the nonpersons of Gilead. Although *The Handmaid's Tale* is fiction, the story echoes narratives that have played out in human history wherein elites have perceived reading as potentially subversive and purposefully kept their subordinates illiterate (for example, in antebellum Southern slaveholding states). In the religious realm, elite men have long held tightly to the keys to biblical (and other scriptural) interpretation. Indeed, although wo/men have made inroads into the church and academy, it is still mostly elite men who read their Revised Standard Versions to Christians in liturgical celebrations and students in academic lectures.

Atwood's narrative illustrates kyriarchal power and prejudice as the political context not only of scholarly discourse on scripture but also of the discourses of liberation and feminist the*logies in the past thirty years or so. Atwood's futuristic projection of a totalitarian state recreating classic biblical kyriarchy in modern technocratic terms underscores that progressive the*logies cannot afford to engage in a purely apologetic reading of the Bible or to relegate a critical biblical interpretation to "bourgeois" scholarship addressing the question of the nonbeliever. Rather, feminist biblical interpretations and the*logies have to engage in a critical analysis that can lay open the "politics of prejudice" inscribed in sacred scriptures. By making feminist theoretical discourse on kyriarchal prejudice central to my hermeneutical explorations, I invite you to attend to the kyriarchal politics of otherness and subordination inscribed in scriptures and right-wing Christian politics.

---

[44] Margaret Atwood, *The Handmaid's Tale* (New York: Ballantine, 1987), 112–13.

In the last four decades, Christian, Jewish, Muslim, Buddhist, Hindu, indigenous, postbiblical, and Goddess feminists have engaged in discussions of prejudice, articulated theoretical structural analyses, and worked toward a feminist transformation of sacred scriptures and religions.[45] In doing so, we have underscored that in all three so-called Abrahamic religions (Judaism/Christianity and Islam), sacred scriptures and traditions have been formulated and interpreted from the perspective of privileged men and, therefore, reflect neither the perspective nor the experiences of wo/men, the poor, or the enslaved. Religious prohibitions, projections, and pious practices have often served to legitimate the the*logies and ways of behaving that marginalize, silence, exclude, and exploit wo/men and other persons categorized as "subhuman." The feminist discussion on prejudice must, therefore, be solidly anchored in a multifaceted critical interreligious, postcolonial, and antiracist analysis.

Hence, if one does not consciously deconstruct the language of imperial domination in which biblical texts remain caught up, one cannot but valorize and reinscribe such anti-wo/man language. In attempting to rescue holy scripture as anti-imperial literature, defensive arguments tend to overlook that the language of kyriarchy and the violence encoded in Jewish and Christian scriptures have shaped Christian religious self-understanding and cultural ethos throughout the centuries, and still do so today.

Such language of domination, subordination, and control is not just historical language. Rather, as sacred scripture, it is performative language that determines Christian identity and praxis. It does not need just to be understood but must be made conscious and critically deconstructed, since the language of "power over" encoded in holy scriptures has two reference points: the Near Eastern and Roman Empires as sociohistorical context and geographical locations of biblical stories, on the one hand, and contemporary forms of antidemocratic discourses on the other.

---

[45] See the special section "Comparative Feminist Hermeneutics," *Journal of Feminist Studies in Religion* 30, no. 2 (Fall 2014): 57–129, which includes the work of Karen Derris (Buddhism), Rachel Adelman (Judaism), Karen Pechilis (Hinduism), and Aysha Hidayatullah (Islam).

Christian religion and scriptures have been used consistently for legitimating Western expansionism and military rule as well as for inculcating the mentality of obedience and submission to antidemocratic powers. The form of biblical and religious legitimization most closely associated with colonialism and the second-class citizenship of wo/men has been hierarchical Catholicism and fundamentalist Protestantism, both of which preach personal submission either to the hierarchy or to the literalist authority of scripture. This ethos of kyriarchal subordination and inferiority is inscribed as divine revelation in sacred scriptures.

The New* Testament texts of subordination have erroneously been classified as "household codes"—a label derived from Lutheran teaching on social status and roles (*Ständelehre*).[46] However, these texts are concerned not only with three sets of household relationships of the same *kyrios* (wife and husband, slave and master, and father and son) but also with submission to the emperor.[47] The cen-

---

[46] Dieter Lührmann, "Wo man nicht mehr Sklave und Freier ist: Überlegungen zur Struktur frühchristlicher Gemeinden," *Wort und Dienst* 13 (1975): 53–83; Klaus Thraede, "Aerger mit der Freiheit: Die Bedeutung von Frauen in Theorie und Praxis der alten Kirche," *Freunde in Christus werden*, ed. Gerda Scharffenroth (Gelnhausen and Berlin: Burckhardthaus, 1977), 35–182; and Clarice Martin, "The *Haustafeln* (Household Codes) in African American Biblical Interpretation: 'Free Slaves' and 'Subordinate Women,'" in *Stony the Road We Trod: African American Biblical Interpretation*, ed. Cain Hope Felder (Minneapolis, MN: Fortress, 1991), 206–31. For a Christological justification of this pattern of subordination, see Else Kähler, *Die Frau in den Paulinischen Briefen* (Zürich: Gotthelf Verlag, 1960). For a feminist evangelical interpretation of the pattern as a pattern of "mutual submission," see, for example, Virginia Ramey Mollenkott, *Women, Men, and the Bible* (Nashville, TX: Abingdon, 1977); Letha Scanzoni and Nancy Hardesty, *All We're Meant to Be: A Biblical Approach to Women's Liberation* (Waco, TX: Word Books, 1975); Esther Yue L. Ng, *Reconstructing Christian Origins? The Feminist Theology of Elisabeth Schüssler Fiorenza: An Evaluation* (Carlisle, PA: Paternoster, 2002); Virginia Ramey Molenkott, "Emancipative Elements in Ephesians 5, 21–33: Why Feminist Scholarship Has (Often) Left Them Unmentioned, and Why They Should Be Emphasized," in *A Feminist Companion to the Deutero-Pauline Epistles*, ed. Amy-Jill Levine (New York: Continuum, 2003), 37–58; David M Scholer, "Tim 2,9–15 and the Place of Women in the Church's Ministry," in Levine, *Feminist Companion to the Deutero-Pauline Epistles*, 98–121.

[47] The code is said to be completely incorporated in Col 3:18–4:1 and Eph 5:22–6:9. However, as in 1 Pet 2:18–3:7 it is not found completely in the remaining passages: 1 Tim 2:11–15; 5:3–8; 6:1–2; Titus 2:2–10; 3:1–2; 1 Clement 21:6–8; Ignatius to Polycarp 4:1–6:2; Didache 4:9–11; Barnabas 19:5–7. Hence, it would be better to call it the "pattern of submission" that can be used in various circumstances.

tral interest of these texts lies both in enforcing the submission and obedience of the socially dependent, weaker group—wives, slaves, and children, the whole community—and in bolstering the authority of the head of the household, the *paterfamilias*, which in the case of the emperor encompassed the whole empire.[48] This model of household and state persists today, and is seen, for example, undergirding legislation such as the Defense of [Heterosexual] Marriage Act, which was formulated against the claim to equal rights of same-sex partners but which the Supreme Court recently rejected by making marriage equality the law of the land.[49] However, at the same time, states have introduced so-called religious freedom legislation that in the name of religion justifies discrimination against LGBT people and undermines wo/men's reproductive choices and rights to healthcare.[50]

The ethos of submission conceives of not only family but also church and state in terms of the kyriarchal household. It gives the kyrios, the lord, slave master, father, and/or husband, power over the members of the household based on scriptural authority that makes people pliant to domination. Hence, I started to analyze and question these texts in the late 1970s and have continued to do so, because their ethos activates not only the Christian but also the political and Religious Right on the whole, since a similar ethos is also at play in other religions.

These texts compel religious wo/men who suffer from both globalized market capitalism and sexual exploitation not to struggle against such death-dealing injustice but to submit to it. The systemic inequality, abuse, violence, discrimination, starvation, poverty, neglect, and denial of wo/men's rights that afflict and disadvantage wo/men around the globe are extensively and statistically

---

[48] Ronald Syme, *The Roman Revolution* (Oxford: Oxford University Press, 1939), 509–24.

[49] Ariane de Vogue and Jeremy Diamond, "Supreme Court Rules in Favor of Same-Sex Marriage Nationwide," *CNN*, June 27, 2015, http://www.cnn.com/2015/06/26/politics/supreme-court-same-sex-marriage-ruling/.

[50] See, for example, the controversial Restoration of Religious Freedom Act. Garrett Epps, "What Makes Indiana's Religious Freedom Law Different?" *The Atlantic*, March 30, 2015, http://www.theatlantic.com/politics/archive/2015/03/what-makes-indianas-religious-freedom-law-different/388997/.

documented.[51] Wo/men still earn only two-thirds of what men in similar situations earn; the majority of people living in poverty are wo/men; violence against wo/men and gynecide (the killing of wo/men) is on the increase; and sexual trafficking, forced labor, illiteracy, migration, and refugee camps spell out globally wo/men's increasing exploitation.

To conclude, I have argued in this chapter that a feminist gender analysis does not suffice to understand either the sociopolitical marker "woman" or the ravages of kyriarchal globalization on wo/men's lives. What is necessary is a kyriarchal analysis of globalization. The system of global domination is best articulated as kyriarchy, rather than as patriarchy or domination of one gender over the other. Insofar as ancient kyriarchy is inscribed in the Bible and in Christian traditions, Christian scriptures and traditions can be used to religiously justify contemporary kyriarchal neoliberal globalization.

To recap my articulation of the social system of kyriarchy, I will try to sum it up with the help of Lynn Weber's intersectional framework.[52]

- Kyriarchy is historically and geographically contextual. Taking a broad historical and global view allows one to register change over time and place.
- Kyriarchy is socially constructed and not biologically determined. It is not engendered by biological imperative, inherent inferiority, or by immutable facts or ordained by G*d.
- Economic, social, and religious kyriarchal relationships are power relationships of dominance and subordination. Here the distinction between personal and social-institutionalized power is central. It is important to ask: How do people come to believe and internalize that they have no power in certain situations?

---

[51] See Jimmy Carter, *A Call to Action: Women, Religion, Violence, and Power* (New York: Simon and Schuster, 2014).
[52] Weber, *Understanding Race, Class, Gender, and Sexuality*, 129–31.

- Kyriarchal economic, social, and religious systems operate both on the macro-level of social institutions and the micro-level of individual life. When analyzing a situation, seeing the psychological manifestations of oppression is much easier than recognizing broad macro-level forces, which are more remote and abstract.

In short, kyriarchal structures are interlocking axes of economic, social, and religious power. They operate to shape people's lives, imaginations, communities, and societies simultaneously. Hence, one needs to analyze not only the one most obvious structure in the foreground (such as gender) but also all structures of domination simultaneously. Thus, progressive and religious communities and persons face a the*-ethical-political choice today. We can strengthen the power of neoliberal kyriarchal globalization or we can support the growing interdependence of people around the globe in and through alternative globalization "from below." We can spiritually sustain the exploitation of capitalist globalization, or we can engage the possibilities of radical democratization for greater freedom, justice, and solidarity.

Religions can inspire individuals and groups to support the forces of economic and cultural global dehumanization, or they can abandon their kyriarchal tendencies and together envision and work for a feminist spiritual ethos of global justice. Either we can foster fundamentalism, exclusivism, and the exploitation of a totalitarian global monoculture or we can advocate radical democratic, spiritual values and visions that celebrate diversity, multiplicity, decision-making power, equality, justice, and well-being for all. Such a the*-ethical-political either/or choice does not reinscribe the dualisms created by structures of domination but struggles to overcome and abolish them. It calls religious wo/men to take sides in the global struggles for greater justice and freedom and for the well-being of wo/men and all of creation. It calls feminist scholars in religion not to analyze gender in isolation but as always already intertwined with other structures of kyriarchal dehumanization and violence.

CHAPTER 2

Essentializing Gender—Theologizing the Feminine

I n Chapter 1, I argued that gender is an integral part of the overar-
ching socioeconomic system of global exploitation in neoliberal
kyriarchy. Globalization "from above" has engendered a situation in
which the majority of the world's poor are wo/men and children
dependent on wo/men.[1] At the same time, democratic grassroots
movements have also been mobilized against this globalization
"from above." Feminist grassroots movements around the globe are
struggling against such globalization and for wo/men's full citizen
rights and well-being. Full citizen rights, they argue, must include
wo/men's reproductive rights, which require the power to decide their
own future and that of their children.

Grassroots antiglobalization movements are inspired by the radical
democratic vision that all people living in this global world-society
should have equal citizenship status. In theory, all citizens of this world
society are created equal, in rights, speech, and power; they are created in
the Divine image. To achieve such a radical egalitarian society of equal
rights and well-being, those who enjoy privileges of race, class, or gender
cannot remain disengaged and detached but must engage in practices
that promote the well-being of all without exception.

---

[1] See Inderpal Grewal, *Transnational America: Feminisms, Diasporas, Neoliberalisms*
(Durham, NC: Duke University Press, 2005).

We must not overlook, however, that religions do not always promote such universal rights and well-being. For example, leaders of the Religious Right have played key roles in promoting neoliberal capitalism and undermining the feminist gains wo/men have made over the past fifty years.[2] For instance, in the United States, right-wing Christian wo/men greatly contributed to the defeat of the Equal Rights Amendment in the 1970s and have become leading "spokesmen" in the last three decades for curtailing wo/men's reproductive rights.[3] The Republican Party's "war on women," which is directed against poor wo/men's reproductive rights, is also supported by right-wing religious wo/men.[4]

To shed light on this perceived "feminist contradiction," I will discuss the structural and subject positions of wo/men in Western kyriarchal democracy to show how structures of domination and power differences are co-constitutive of the essentialist gender identity formation of wo/men. A critical feminist the*logy understands such

---

[2] See John Stratton Hawley, ed., *Fundamentalism and Gender* (New York: Oxford University Press, 1994), especially Karen McCarthy Brown, "Fundamentalism and the Control of Women," 175–201. See also Christel Manning, *God Gave Us the Right: Conservative Catholic, Evangelical Protestant, and Orthodox Jewish Women Grapple with Feminism* (New Brunswick, NJ: Rutgers University Press, 1999).

[3] The Equal Rights Amendment passed by Congress in 1972 would have become the twenty-seventh amendment to the Constitution if three-fourths of the states had ratified it by June 30, 1982. However, that date passed with only thirty-five of the necessary thirty-eight state ratifications. Instead, the 27th Amendment is the Madison Amendment, concerning Congressional pay raises, which went to the states for ratification in 1972 and reached the three-fourths goal in 1992. See "The ERA: A Brief Introduction," http://www.equalrightsamendment.org/overview.htm.http://www.google.com/url?url=http://webcache.googleusercontent.com/search%3Fhl%3Den%26biw%26bih%26q%3Dcache:ymowIFCuBy4J:http://www.equalrightsamendment.org/overview.htm%252Bequal%2Brights%2Bamendment%26gbv%3D2%26%26ct%3Dclnk&rct=j&frm=1&q=&esrc=s&sa=U&ei=UeqXVdGLBsnstQWZ35mYDg&ved=0CCQQIDAC&usg=AFQjCNGRdVjxcC9p4-8tyQ-_dfmH9qLdYghttps://www.google.com/search?hl=en&gbv=2&q=related:www.equalrightsamendment.org/overview.htm+equal+rights+amendment&tbo=1&sa=X&ei=UeqXVdGLBsnstQWZ35mYDg&ved=0CCUQHzAC.

[4] The Republican "war" on wo/men's reproductive rights is part and parcel of global violence. See especially Susan Brooks Thistlethwaite, *Women's Bodies as Battlefields: Christian Theology and the Global War on Women* (New York: Palgrave Macmillan, 2015). See also Carter, *Call to Action*.

identity constructs not in essentialist terms but as effects of power generated by identity categories that are naturalized and essentialized in Christian the*logical terms.

While the essentialized and essentializing New Feminism has actively organized a right-wing wo/men's movement in the past decades, feminist liberation the*logies and studies in religion have focused on the academic study of religion and the*logy and concentrated on wo/men's ordination or on same-sex marriage. We have neglected to create educational community spaces for feminist the*logical knowledge production or have exchanges on the grassroots or global levels that could address this contradiction in wo/men's identity formation.[5] Feminists in religion, therefore, have to develop their work not just in terms of knowledge production but also as a means of communal conscientization.[6]

Kyriarchal Identity Formation and Global Struggles for Wo/men's Rights

As we have seen, the modern, elite, male, liberal model of democracy was pioneered in Ancient Greece.[7] This model was not constructed in abstract and universal terms but was rooted in a concrete sociopolitical situation. Greek kyriarchal democracy constituted itself through the exclusion of those "others" who did not have a share in the land but whose labor sustained society. Freedom and citizenship were not only measured over and against slavery but also restricted in terms of gender.

---

5 For example, see Kathryn Joice, *Quiverfull: Inside the Christian Patriarchy Movement* (Boston: Beacon, 2009).

6 For such attempts, see Elisabeth Schüssler Fiorenza, *Los Caminos de la Sabiduria: Una Introducción a la interpretación feminista de la Biblia* (Santander, Spain: Sal Terrae, 2004), and Elisabeth Schüssler Fiorenza, *Democratizing Biblical Studies: Toward an Emancipatory Educational Space* (Louisville, KY: Westminster John Knox, 2009).

7 See, for example, Moller Okin, *Women in Western Political Thought*; Christine DiStephano, *Configurations of Masculinity: A Feminist Perspective on Modern Political Theory* (Ithaca, NY: Cornell University Press, 1991); or Susan Hekman, *The Feminine Subject* (Cambridge: Polity, 2014), 77–112.

Moreover, the socioeconomic realities in the Greek city-states were such that only a select few freeborn, propertied, elite male heads of households could actually participate in democratic government. The attempt to equalize the situation by paying male citizens without sufficient wealth of their own for participating in government could not eliminate the existing tension between the ideal of equality and the kyriarchal structuring of society. Participation in government remained conditional upon not only citizenship but also the combined privileges of property, education, and freeborn male family status on which citizenship depended.

Feminist political theorists have shown that the writings of both Aristotle and Plato, our main sources for understanding ancient democracy, articulate in different ways theories of kyriarchal democracy in order to justify why certain groups of people, such as freeborn citizen wo/men or slave wo/men, were not capable of participating in democratic government.[8] These groups of people were not fit to rule or to decide the affairs of the commonwealth because of their allegedly deficient natural powers of reasoning. Such explicit ideological justifications of exclusion always seem necessary at those points in history when it becomes increasingly obvious that those who are excluded from politics—such as freeborn wo/men, educated slave wo/men, or wealthy alien resident wo/men—are indispensable to it.[9]

A similar contradiction between democratic vision and sociopolitical reality became evident with the emergence of modern Western democracies, which have articulated themselves as *fraternal* capitalist

---

[8] See, especially, Okin, *Women in Western Political Thought*; Page DuBois, *Centaurs and Amazons: Women and the Pre-History of the Great Chain of Being* (Ann Arbor: University of Michigan Press, 1982), Page DuBois, *Torture and Truth* (London: Routledge, 1991); Mary E. Hawkesworth, *Beyond Oppression: Feminist Theory and Political Strategy* (New York: Continuum, 1990); Eva C. Keuls, *The Reign of the Phallus: Sexual Politics in Ancient Athens* (New York: Harper and Row, 1985); and A. Rouselle, *Porneia: On Desire and the Body in Antiquity* (New York: Basil Blackwell, 1988). Compare with Christine Faure, *Democracy without Women* (Bloomington: Indiana University Press, 1991).
[9] Please remember that I use wo/men as inclusive of men.

kyriarchies.[10] Since modern capitalist democracy is modeled after the classical ideal of kyriarchal democracy, it has perpetuated the contradiction between the kyriarchal practices of exclusion and subjection inscribed in the discourses of democracy in antiquity. At first, modern democracy excluded propertied, freeborn wo/men, "the ladies," as well as immigrant, poor, and slave wo/men from the democratic rights of citizenship. "Property" and elite male status by birth and education, not simply biological-cultural masculinity, entitled one to participate in the government of the few over the many.

We must not overlook, however, that this institutionalized contradiction between the ideals of radical democracy and their kyriarchal actualization has also engendered emancipation movements for those seeking full self-determining citizenship. In the past centuries, these emancipatory struggles have won voting and civil rights for all adult citizens. These movements, however, have not been able to overcome the kyriarchal stratifications that continue to determine modern constitutional democracies; they merely made the democratic circle coextensive with the kyriarchal pyramid, thereby reinscribing the contradiction between democratic vision and political kyriarchal practices. In the process, democratic liberty is construed merely as the absence of coercion, and the democratic process is reduced to the spectacle of election campaigns.

As I pointed out in the previous chapter, in the context of classical and modern kyriarchal democracies, female gender identity has been constructed in terms of the "lady" as essential feminine identity. The lady was subordinated to the gentleman head of household, but she still had power over his family, workers, servants, and slave wo/men. In short, masculine gender identity has been articulated in antiquity and modernity in terms of the headship and ruling power of

---

10 See, for example, Genevieve Lloyd, *The Man of Reason: "Male" and "Female" in Western Philosophy* (Minneapolis: University of Minnesota Press, 1984); Robin May Schott, *Cognition and Eros: A Critique of the Kantian Paradigm* (Boston: Beacon, 1988); and Linda J. Nicholson, *Feminism/Postmodernism* (New York: Routledge, 1990).

the elite male, the *kyrios*, whereas feminine gender identity has been defined in terms of the submission, service, and love of the elite wo/man, the *kyria*. Elite wo/men and their children were subordinated and dependent on the male heads of households, who were to represent them in the democratic public.

In industrialized modern societies, as heads of households all men had to earn a family wage to fulfill their masculine calling, whereas middle- and upper-class wo/men had the privilege to "stay at home," take care of the household, and fulfill their educational and civilizing calling in and through motherhood. However, wo/men of color or lower-class wo/men never had the privilege to stay home and take care of their own families because, as slaves and servants, they had to take care of the house and children of the lady. This status and class or racial inflection of gender and identity is often overlooked when gender is essentialized and intersectionality is not taken into account.

In short, the philosophical articulation of the logic of identity in antiquity defined the asymmetric binary dualisms of human-animal, male-female, and free-slave as "natural" differences in order to legitimate kyriarchal relations of domination and subjection. Modern democracy perpetrates many of the ideological practices found in ancient political philosophy insofar as it claims that its citizens are "created equal" and are entitled to "liberty, and the pursuit of happiness," while it retains "natural" kyriarchal sociopolitical stratifications. This classical kyriarchal discourse is inscribed in Christian scriptures, rearticulated in Christian the*logy, and reproduced in modern political science. This discourse emerges in various ways: it manifests itself in the Enlightenment philosophers' construction of the "Man of Reason," it surfaces in Euro-American racist gender discourses on the White Lady, and it inhabits the Western colonialist construction of "inferior races" and "uncivilized savages" for which Christian religion was considered to be a "civilizing" force.

Status Position and Subject Formation

Since *identity* and *subjectivity* are constructed and made common sense by this colonial politics of domination and subordination in modern capitalist democracies, I prefer a *status* rather than an *identity* model of social organization for developing a social analytic of kyriarchy. Such an analytic examines the intersecting institutionalized structures and value patterns of domination for their effects on the relative status of social actors both in a given society and in a text. If such status inscriptions constitute persons as peers capable of participating on par with each other, then we can speak of status equality or grassroots democracy. If they are not able to do so, then we speak of kyriarchal domination or democracy.

We interpret the social structures in which we are positioned through cultural, political, and religious discourses. Since we cannot stand outside the interpretive frameworks available in our society and time, we "make sense" of life with their help. For instance, one wo/man might be influenced by neoliberalism and believe that her social position results from the fact that she worked harder in life than the wo/man on welfare who lives down the street. Another wo/man influenced by right-wing religious fundamentalism might explain her situation with the fact that she is blessed by G*d because of her virtuous life, whereas the unmarried mother on welfare has gravely sinned and, therefore, is punished with poverty. Again, another wo/man might believe that her success as a wife and mother is due to her feminine attractiveness and selfless dedication to her husband and children, and that the fate of poor wo/men is due to their lack thereof.

If we always have to resort to existing interpretive discourses to make sense of our lives or of cultural and religious texts, then the importance of social movements for justice becomes obvious. Since malestream hegemonic discourses provide the frameworks in which we "make meaning" in kyriarchal situations, feminist theory and the*logy need to provide discourses that illuminate not only the choreography of oppression but also the possibilities for a radical democratic society and religion. Yet, we are able to articulate an emancipatory self-understanding and worldview only within the context of radical democratic social movements that shape theories that help us exploit the contradictions existing between diverse socio-hegemonic discourses and envision an alternative sociopolitical-religious world.

Structural Position

For doing so, I have found the distinction between a person's *structural position* and her *subject position* important. Every individual is *structurally* positioned within social, cultural, economic, political, and religious systems by virtue of birth. No one can choose to be born white, black, Asian, European, mixed race, poor, healthy, male, or female. We always find ourselves already positioned by and within structures of domination that limit the chances we get in life. For example, wo/men are not poor or homeless because we have low motivation, faulty self-esteem, or poor work habits. Rather, wo/men are poor or homeless because of our *structural position* within intersecting relations of domination such as gender, class, race, or corporality.

In her work, María Lugones argues that it is the "coloniality of power" that defines our structural positions. She has borrowed this term from Peruvian sociologist Anibal Quijano, who understands "coloniality of power" as violently defining the intersecting structural positions of gender, race, and class. Lugones contends that heterosexism is a key avenue through which gender fuses with race, and it does so in the operations of colonial power.[11] Furthermore, she argues that many who have taken the coloniality of power seriously have naturalized gender and overlooked the "deep imbrication of race, gender, class, and sexuality."[12] Lugones discusses Quijano's concept and points out that "Quijano's framework

---

[11] Lugones, "Heterosexualism and the Colonial/Modern Gender System." 186–209.
[12] Ibid., 187.

restricts gender to the organization of sex. . . . Quijano appears to take for granted that the dispute over control of sex is a dispute among men, about men's control of resources which are thought to be female."[13]

Referring to Oyéronké Oyewùmi's research on Yoruba society, Lugones argues that the West has used binary gender constructions as a tool of domination.[14] Following the argument of Paula Gunn Allen on Native American peoples, she points out that such oppressive use of colonial gender as a weapon destroyed their two-sided complementary social structure, which included a female chief administering internal affairs and a male chief responsible for mediating among the tribes and outsiders. According to Gunn Allen, the introduction of the binary heterosexual gender system was the colonial tool used to co-opt colonized men into kyriarchal roles and undermine the wo/men's social power.[15] Lugones concludes, "It should be clear by now that the colonial, modern gender system cannot exist without the coloniality of power, since the classification of the population in terms of race is a necessary condition of its possibility."[16]

Lugones rightly claims that the heterosexist gender system exercises control over not only sex but also over labor and other resources. However, she does not pay much attention as to how this gender system both co-opts men and has also colonized middle- and upper-class wo/men, the "ladies," to perform the coloniality of power or, as I would say, the kyriarchality of power. In short, identity categories such as gender, race, class, and corporality are best understood as power effects engendered by the structures of domination and articulated in essentialist ontological terms. Their structural intersections inculcate unequal social identity differences and essentialist gender inequalities.

---

[13] Ibid., 194.

[14] Oyéronké Oyewùmi, *The Invention of Women: Making an African Sense of Western Gender Discourses* (Minneapolis: University of Minnesota Press, 1997).

[15] Paula Gunn Allen, *The Sacred Hoop: Recovering the Feminine in American Indian Traditions* (Boston: Beacon, 1986). See also the website in memory of her, "Paula Gunn Allen Online Memorial," www.paulagunnallen.net/.

[16] Gunn Allen, *Sacred Hoop*, 202.

Subject Position

Unlike a *structural position*, a *subject position* is variable, open to intervention, and changeable but also limited by the coloniality of power expressed in hegemonic structures of domination.[17] According to theorists Ernest Laclau and Chantal Mouffe, "a 'subject position' refers to the ensemble of beliefs through which an individual interprets and responds to her structural positions within a social formation. In this sense, an individual becomes a social agent insofar as she lives her structural positions through an ensemble of subject positions."[18]

The relationship between a subject position and a structural position is complex since our self-understandings are always already determined by our structural position with its rewards and pressures. Thus, a person might theoretically be able to live her structural positions through a wide range of subject positions but practically be restricted to a rigidly defined and closed set of available interpretive frameworks. Hence, the importance of emancipatory movements and the different interpretive frameworks they articulate is clear.

Feminist theories and the*logies have made available a wide range of such interpretive frameworks and categories for shaping wo/men's subject positions. They have provided various social analytics for diagnosing and changing wo/men's structural positions in and through the articulation of different subject positions. Key analytic concepts and categories with which to think in a feminist fashion have been developed either as reverse discourse to the binary intellectual framework of systemic dualisms or in a critical liberationist frame.

---

[17] "What had been experienced as personal failings are socially produced conflicts and contradictions shared by many women in similar social positions. This process of discovery can lead to a rewriting of personal experience in terms which give it social, changeable causes" (Chris Weedon, *Feminist Practice and Poststructuralist Theory* [Malden, MA: Blackwell, 1987], 33).

[18] Anna Marie Smith, *Laclau, and Mouffe: The Radical Democratic Imaginary* (New York: London, 1998), 58–59.

Feminist analytic categories such as gender, intersectionality, coloniality of power, or kyriarchy seek to provide alternative theoretical spaces from which to critically analyze our structural position and articulate, in tandem with such critical analyses and constructive alternative visions, the range of possible subject positions. Fixed identity definitions and essentialist conceptions, conversely, keep us in the kyriarchal spaces the powers of subjection provide.

How essentializing and naturalizing identity constructions seek to maintain and reinforce kyriarchal subject positions and mind-sets of inequality can be seen when one pays close attention to the discourses of New Feminism or True Woman in Christian religion. These discourses and movements seek to persuade wo/men to inhabit their structural feminine gender position in religious terms. It is not surprising that especially white middle-class wo/men, the ladies, have been attracted to such the*logies of wo/manhood and have adopted them as revealed feminine subject positions.

Gender Essentialism and the Religious Right

Feminist philosopher Susan Hekman has reviewed feminist discussions of the feminine subject.[19] In her work, she provides a concise and clearly written discussion that moves from Simone de Beauvoir's "woman is not born but made" to French feminism, "radical" feminism, liberalism, Marxism, postmodernism, and intersectionality to Butler's material subject and the move from difference to differences to eco-politics and finally to materialist feminism, which Hekman sees not as "a conclusion but as the springboard for the next iteration of 'woman.'"[20] Interestingly, though, Hekman does not discuss the "feminine" in religious discourses.

While feminist theorists have hotly debated gender essentialism, difference, complementarity, the ethics of care, and radical feminism, they have paid very little attention to the dualistic, feminine identity movements and the*logies in Christianity and their differing kyriarchal

---

[19] Hekman, *Feminine Subject*.
[20] Ibid., 185.

constructions of the Eternal Woman or "feminine genius" as the subject position of white upper-class femininity.[21] Whereas the Protestant True Woman movement is biblically based, the Roman Catholic New Feminism movement is inspired by the the*logy of woman Pope John Paul II formulated.[22] Both essentialist theologies and movements are articulated in order to counteract the influence of feminist egalitarian the*logies and liberation movements. The New Feminism has taken over many feminist liberationist arguments and movement strategies in order to foster the cultural bourgeois femininity of the White Lady.

The New Feminism[23]

The term New Feminism was originally used in 1920s England to differentiate suffragist feminism and the "new" feminism, which was primarily concerned with motherhood and family. Pope John Paul II reintroduced the term in Evangelium Vitae (1995). Just as he had called for a "new" liberation the*logy, so too he called for a "new feminist theology." Hence, John Paul II sought to promote New Feminism and the "genius" of woman over and against feminist liberation the*logy. According to him, the New Feminism rejects models of "male domination" and insists on woman's true essence, which is biological and spiritual motherhood. While John Paul II stressed the human dignity of woman as a person, he conceptualized this dignity of male and female not as equality but as complementarity. Man and woman are essentially different, but such difference enables them to complement each other.

It has been shown that since the nineteenth century, official Roman Catholic teachings have developed in interaction with the feminist movement worldwide. These teachings have stressed, in line

---

[21] See, for example, Natalie Stoljar, "Essentialism," in Code, Encyclopedia of Feminist Theories, 177–78; and Naomi Schor and Elizabeth Weed, eds., The Essential Difference (Bloomington: Indiana University Press, 1994).

[22] See Rita Perinfalvi, ed., Women and Religion: Dignity of the Woman as Dignity of the Human Being (Cluj-Napoca: Verbum, 2011), esp. 13–32 (E. Adamiak) and 145–56 (J. A. Melonowska).

[23] More recently under Pope Francis, the Vatican proclaims the "feminine genius."

with Augustine and Thomas Aquinas, the equivalence of the genders but at the same time have insisted on the subordination of wo/men.[24] Beginning in the 1960s and especially during the reign of John Paul II, this official Roman Catholic rhetoric changed, however, from emphasizing "subordination" to stressing "complementarity." The sexes are different but equal and complement each other. Wo/men and men are equal in rational capacity and dignity, and are created in the image and likeness of G*d. Hence, they deserve equal respect and dignity as human beings. They are to change the unequal status of wo/men and men in society, but not in the church, whose hierarchical structures are divinely ordained to be male gendered.

However, as Ivy Helman asserts, wo/men's structural and subject positions are "sexed and gendered down to their souls. Femininity is not just something women do; it is something women are. . . . Being feminine means taking on God's divine design for women."[25] Femininity operates out of "the order of love" and is fulfilled either in physical or spiritual motherhood. Thus altruism, service, self-sacrifice, care, sensitivity, and authentic love are natural capacities of wo/men as G*d created them. On grounds of their G*d-given nature, wo/men excel by devoting their lives to others either in the family or in society. They are called to teach men the virtues of love and service that are not naturally given to the masculine gender.

The *New Feminism* is articulated to engender a right-wing Roman Catholic wo/men's movement in support of the Vatican's societal and ecclesiastical anti-wo/man politics.[26] It is often overlooked that John

---

[24] Kari Elisabeth Børresen, *Subordination and Equivalence: The Nature and Role of Woman in Augustine and Thomas Aquinas* (Washington, DC: University Press of America, 1981).

[25] Ivy A. Helman, *Women and the Vatican: An Exploration of Official Documents* (New York: Orbis, 2012), 103.

[26] For its intellectual justification, see Michele M. Schumacher, ed., *Women in Christ: Toward a New Feminism* (Grand Rapids, MI: Eerdmans, 2003); Elizabeth Fox Genovese, *Feminism Is Not the Story of My Life: How Today's Feminist Elite Has Lost Touch with the Real Concerns of Women* (New York: Doubleday, 1996); Gloria Conde, *Mujer nueva: Ellas: Hay una pequena diferencia*, trans. Karna Swanson (New York: Circle Press, 2002); and Karen Doyle, *The Genius of Womanhood* (Boston, MA: Pauline Books and Media, 2009).

Paul II's rhetoric builds on the rhetoric of the "Eternal Woman," which was inspired by German Romanticism (Goethe: "Das ewig Weibliche zieht uns hinan" ["The eternal feminine draws us heaven- ward"]). Edith Stein (1932) and Gertrud von LeFort (1934), among others, rearticulated this concept in the context of and as a religious alternative to the emerging "new woman" ideology and politics of German National Socialism.[27] Both authors emphasized that wo/men's essence and vocation comprised biological and spiritual motherhood.[28]

Read as a response to technological developments and the inter- national feminist movements, the Vatican's lofty the*logy of woman- hood turns out to be articulated as kyriarchal ideology of the (White) Lady justifying the hierarchy's stance on birth control, termination of pregnancy, and the exclusion of wo/men from church office. As in Nazi Germany, so also in today's official Roman Catholicism, right- wing women and women's movements are inspired by the the*logy of the Eternal Woman to spread its lofty but oppressive message among wo/men.[29]

Feminist struggles for wo/men's reproductive rights, access and right to birth control, and safe termination of pregnancy as well as the feminist insistence on wo/men's rights to participate in the decision- making and sacramental powers of the Church's ministry have thus

---

[27] Renate Bridenthal, Anita Grossmann, and Marion Kaplan, *When Biology Became Destiny* (New York: New Feminist Library, 1984); and Claudia Koonz, *Mothers in the Fatherland: Women, the Family, and Nazi Politics* (New York: Routledge, 1986). Koonz and Bridenthal established that the leaders of German feminist groups were happy to go along with "Gleichschaltung," a policy that sought to bring about adherence to a specific doctrine and way of thinking and to control as many aspects of life as possi- ble. Female supporters of the Nazis accepted the Nazi division of the sexes into a pub- lic sphere for men and a private sphere for women.

[28] See Schüssler Fiorenza, *Der Vergessene Partner* (Düsseldorf: Patmos Verlag, 1964).

[29] See, for example, Women for Faith and Family, http://www.wf-f.org; Women of the Third Millennium, http://wttm.org/about.html); and ENDOW: Educating on the Nature and Dignity of Women, established in the Archdiocese of Denver, http://endowgroups.org/about-us/the-mission/. "New Feminism" is defined by Pope John Paul II and recognizes and affirms the "true genius of women" and responds to our culture's desperate need for an authentic feminine presence in every aspect of life and society.

engendered the Vatican's articulation of the *New Feminism*.[30] After Pope John XXIII endorsed religious freedom and a range of civil rights also for wo/men in his *Encyclical Pacem in Terries* (1963)[31] and the assembly of bishops in Vatican II, the struggles for reproductive and ecclesial rights have become the central Catholic feminist struggles post-Vatican II. In the context of the increasing willingness to ordain wo/men in Protestant churches, wo/men's ordination has become a controverted right also for Roman Catholic wo/men.

A birth-control commission appointed during Vatican II delivered its report to Pope Paul VI in June 1966, which was passed by a commission vote of 52 to 4. The commission's majority recommended that any method of contraception within a framework of committed love was acceptable as long as it was medically and psychologically sound, whereas the minority insisted that the authority of the traditional teaching was infallible. Paul VI, who was worried about weakening the hierarchy's teaching authority, sided with the minority in his 1968 encyclical *Humanae Vitae*.[32] However, the opposite turned out to be the case. The encyclical severely relativized and undermined the teaching authority of the hierarchy insofar as most Catholics and clergy rejected the papal teaching in light of their own informed conscience based on the the*logical arguments of the

---

[30] See the excellent book by Patricia Miller, *Good Catholics: The Battle over Abortion in the Catholic Church* (Berkeley: University of California Press, 2014), which tells the history of those who have engaged in a nearly fifty-year struggle to assert the moral legitimacy of a pro-choice position. However, I miss the story of Latin American Catholic feminists who more appropriately named their movement as Our Right to Decide (Católicas por el Derecho a Decidir [CDD], http://www.catolicasporelderechoadecidir.net/inicio.php) although the CDD Latin America network was established in 1987 in collaboration with US "Catholics for a Free Choice." I prefer the rights-language over "choice" formulations because "choice" language resonates too much with neoliberal consumer language.

[31] Pope John XXIII, "Pacem in Terris, Encyclical on Establishing Universal Peace in Truth, Justice, Charity, and Liberty," April 11, 1963, http://w2.vatican.va/content/john-xxiii/en/encyclicals/documents/hf_j-xxiii_enc_11041963_pacem.html.

[32] "Encyclical Letter, Humanae Vitae of the Supreme Pontiff, Paul VI, to His Venerable Brothers the Patriarchs, Archbishops, Bishops, and Other Local Ordinaries in Peace and Communion with the Apostolic See, to the Clergy and Faithful of the Whole Catholic World, and to All Men of Good Will, on the Regulation of Birth," *The Pope Speaks* 13 (Fall 1969): 329–46, http://w2.vatican.va/content/paul-vi/en/encyclicals/documents/hf_p-vi_enc_25071968_humanae-vitae.html.

majority of the papal commission and of the*logians around the world.

Whereas Paul VI's successors in the papacy have continued to insist that the traditional teaching on contraception is not only unchangeable but infallible, the majority of Catholics around the world have rejected this teaching. However, one must not overlook that the papal the*logy of womanhood, motherhood, the feminine genius, and complementarity has been developed in the context of this birth-control debate. The Vatican has insisted the*logically on wo/man's essence and nature as biological or spiritual motherhood and has politically attempted, through regional bishops' conferences and its representation at UN conferences, to prevent funding for birth control and abortion for wo/men around the world.[33] To give a recent example: Poland's bishops' conference denounced a Council of Europe Convention aimed at prohibiting violence against wo/men because the government had consulted "only women with leftist views" while ignoring pro-life and family groups. The Polish bishops insisted that the Convention document was erroneous in "defining differences as socially constructed" and "totally ignoring natural biological differences between men and women."[34]

However, the majority of Catholic wo/men has not bought into the papal argument against artificial contraception and has rejected it through their praxis. In the United States, more than 90 percent of Catholics have used or are using contraceptives, and the majority has consistently insisted that abortion remain legal. Recently, Melinda Gates, a practicing Catholic, has made world news announcing her lifelong commitment to providing contraception for wo/men worldwide.[35] She argues that it is necessary that wo/men have the decision-making power to plan and space pregnancies responsibly so that they can feed and

---

[33] See the excellent analysis by Aline H. Kalbian, *Sexing the Church: Gender, Power, and Ethics in Contemporary Catholicism* (Bloomington: Indiana University Press, 2005), 55–93. See also Rosemary Radford Ruether, *Catholic Does Not Equal the Vatican: A Vision for Progressive Catholicism* (New York: The New Press, 2008), 41–59.

[34] *The Tablet*, July 14, 2012, 24.

[35] See Tim Padgett, "Sorry, Rome, U.S. Catholics Are More Like Melinda Gates," July 12, 2012, http://ideas.time.com/2012/07/12/sorry-rome-us-catholics-more-like-melinda-gates/?iid=op-article-mostpop1#ixzz20XJaRjpi.

educate the children to whom they give birth. Studies show that responsible contraceptive use has enabled families to move out of poverty, whereas the lack of effective contraceptive leads to an increase in abortions, starvation, and impoverishment.

In short, the Vatican doctrine of gender complementarity presupposes that maleness and femaleness are essential sex/gender structural positions that exist in a binary opposition. This doctrine does not simply insist on the meaning of gender, but decrees that there are only two distinct genders that are essentially different and that each gender has to complement its opposite. Although this Vatican gender definition insists on the absolute equality of male and female in their complementarity, it nevertheless goes on to say that the primary female/feminine gender function is self-sacrificing motherhood based on wo/men's physical and psychological condition. Wo/men can achieve their full potential either through physical motherhood or through spiritual motherhood, sacrificing themselves for others.

This doctrine of complementarity based on ontological gender differences is also used by the hierarchy to prohibit wo/men's admission to hierarchical church offices through ordination. Because Jesus' maleness is defined in ontological male gender terms, wo/men cannot represent him because they lack his ontological maleness. Their physical-ontological structural gender position entitles men but not wo/men to hold positions of sacred institutional power in the church. Although this doctrine of gender complementarity contradicts the doctrine of incarnation, which does not say that Jesus became male but that Jesus became human, it is enforced as infallible truth.

The True Woman Movement

My second example of gender essentialism derives from a Protestant Evangelical context. Although in the last fifty years variegated right-wing women's movements have emerged, I focus here on one paradigmatic example. The True Woman movement is a worldwide, grassroots movement that, according to its website, was birthed on October 11, 2008, when over six thousand wo/men gathered in

Chicago, Illinois, for the unveiling and signing of the True Woman Manifesto at Revive Our Hearts' first True Woman Conference. The website explains the the*logical grounding:

> The seeds for this movement actually began taking shape in Nancy Leigh DeMoss' heart eleven years earlier. As she read about the historical development of secular and religious feminism in Mary Kassian's book, *The Feminist Mistake*,[36] her spirit was exercised within her. When she realized the powerful lies that had been foisted on a whole generation of women, the pervasiveness of feminist thinking in our whole culture, and the extent to which Christian women have bought into the whole philosophy, she began to ask: If a handful of women have succeeded by their writings and influence in destroying and brainwashing an entire generation with their Godless philosophies, *what could God do with a handful of women who were determined to "reclaim surrendered ground"*?[37]

The statement continues: "Ever since the movement began in 2008, we've been watching God 'reclaim surrendered ground.'" Over twenty thousand women have attended the four True Woman national women's conferences and left energized and equipped to encourage women in their own spheres of influence.[38] In May 2012, the first ever international Revive Our Hearts Conference took place in Santo Domingo, which indicates the movement's intention to spread also into Latin America.[39]

Part of the "True Woman Manifesto" reads:[40]

> As Christian women, we desire to honor God by living counter-cultural lives that reflect the beauty of Christ and His gospel to our world. To that end, we affirm that . . .

---

[36] Mary Kassian, *The Feminist Mistake: The Radical Impact of Feminism and Culture*, 2nd ed. (Wheaton, IL: Crossway, 2005).
[37] http://www.reviveourhearts.com/resource-library
[38] See True Woman, http://www.truewoman.com, emphasis added.
[39] See Revive Our Hearts, http://www.reviveourhearts.com/resource-library.
[40] True Woman Manifesto, http://www.truewoman.com/?id=980.

- Scripture is God's authoritative means of instructing us in His ways and it reveals His holy pattern for our womanhood, our character, our priorities, and our various roles, responsibilities, and relationships.
- Men and women are both created in the image of God and are equal in value and dignity, but they have distinct roles and functions in the home and in the church.
- We are called as women to affirm and encourage men as they seek to express godly masculinity, and to honor and support God-ordained male leadership in the home and in the church.
- Marriage, as created by God, is a sacred, binding, lifelong covenant between one man and one woman.
- When we respond humbly to male leadership in our homes and churches, we demonstrate a noble submission to authority that reflects Christ's submission to God His Father.
- Selfish insistence on personal rights is contrary to the spirit of Christ, who humbled Himself, took on the form of a servant, and laid down His life for us.
- Human life is precious to God and is to be valued and protected, from the point of conception until rightful death.
- Children are a blessing from God; women are uniquely designed to be bearers and nurturers of life, whether it be their own biological or adopted children, or other children in their sphere of influence.
- God's plan for gender is wider than marriage; all women, whether married or single, are to model femininity in their various relationships, by exhibiting a distinctive modesty, responsiveness, and gentleness of spirit.

The complete list of affirmations is much longer, but I have selected those affirmations that are key for the movement's religious gender construction. Whereas the Roman Catholic New Feminism movement and its definition of gender and gender complementarity reasons ontologically, the Protestant Evangelical Radical Womanhood or True Woman movements point to scripture, especially Gen 1–3,

Eph 5, and 1 Tim as preaching gender complementarity.[41] Both movements overlook that "gender complementarity" is a modern Romantic conceptualization of woman and marriage that has replaced the kyriarchal scriptural injunction to subordination and submission as we find them in the so-called Household Code text tradition of the New* Testament, which demands the subordination of wo/men.[42]

Today, the Religious Right not only insists on gender complementarity in heterosexual marriage but also rejects same-sex marriage. Mary Kassian, the True Woman movement's intellectual godmother, however, structures her book not in terms of the gender complementarity argument but rather derives her story from Mary Daly, who wrote forty years ago in *Beyond God the Father* that under patriarchy "women have had the power of naming stolen from us."[43] Daly directed our attention to the second creation story of the book of Genesis in which Adam names all the animals as well as the woman. However, the woman herself names no one and nothing. From this, Daly draws the conclusion that women "are now realizing that the universal imposing of names by men has been false or partial because to exist humanly is to name the self, the world, and G*d."[44]

Yet, wo/men did not simply lack the sacred power of naming because their female natures would not allow them to do so. Rather, this sacred power of naming was actively denied to wo/men. To quote a familiar text of St. Paul:

> As in all the *ekklēsia* (the democratic assemblies) of the saints, the women should keep silence in the *ekklēsia*.

---

[41] See Susanne Scholz, "The Christian Rights Discourse on Gender and the Bible," *Journal of Feminist Studies in Religion* 21, no. 1 (2005): 81–100. See also Susanne Scholz, "The Forbidden Fruit for the New Eve: The Christian Right's Adaptation to the (Post) Modern World," in *Interreligious Hermeneutics in Pluralistic Europe: Between Texts and People*, eds. David Cheetham, Ulrich Winkler, Oddbjørn Lirvik, and Juditth Gruber (Amsterdam: Odopi, 2011), 289–315.

[42] See Schüssler Fiorenza, *In Memory of Her: A Feminist Theological Reconstruction of Christian Origins* (New York: Crossroad, 1983) and *But She Said: Feminist Practices of Biblical Interpretation* (Beacon: Boston, 1992).

[43] Mary Daly, *Beyond God the Father* (Boston: Beacon, 1984).

[44] Ibid., 8.

For they are not permitted to speak,

but should be subordinate, as even the law says.

If there is anything they desire to know,

let them ask their husbands at home.

For it is shameful for a woman to speak in the ekklesia.

What! Did the word of God originate with you,

or are you the only ones it has reached? (1 Cor 14:33–36 RSV)

Or:

Let a woman learn in silence with all submissiveness.

I permit no woman to teach or to have authority over men;

she is to keep silent. (1 Tim 2:11–12 RSV)

Kassian structures her antistory of the feminist movement in three parts following Daly's outline: Stage one: Naming the Self; Stage two: Naming the World; and Stage three: Naming G*d. But she tells it as a success story with disastrous outcomes. According to Kassian, women in the beginning wanted to overcome their biological difference in order to be equal with men, that is, the same as men. Consequently, feminists fought for legalized abortion, changes in marriage law, day care, pay equity, affirmative action, and language changes. In the second phase of naming the world, feminists emphasized their strength and added issues such as homosexual or aboriginal rights, disarmament, and women-centered politics. In the third phase, feminism moved into esoteric spiritualities and an ecological awareness of such issues as pollution, animal rights, and the preservation of rain forests. When feminism reached this third phase in North America, all of the feminist goals of the previous two phases were achieved.[45]

According to Kassian, society accepted all feminist goals: abortion, day care, divorce, sexual liberty, and affirmative action. She

---

[45] Kassian, *Feminist Mistake*, 280–81.

asserts that, like an intravenous drug, feminist thought has so much pervaded our culture that to speak of G*d's gracious design for womanhood becomes very difficult:

> Nowadays, proposing that men are more suited to provide for their families or to be in such occupations as the military, law enforcement, firefighting, or chief executive officers of corporations—or that mothers are more suited to nurture young children—would be tantamount to cultural heresy. . . Intimating that affirmative action and gender quotas are harmful to the workplace or that textbooks could be filled with images of fathers as providers or mothers as caregivers would be met with incredulity. Even within the church, those who believe that God has given men and women unique roles are regarded as outdated.[46]

Feminist Struggles for Reproductive Rights and Church Leadership

Rather than end with this alleged success story of feminism that fuels the the*logy of the religious feminine countermovements, I want to contextualize my reflections in my own sociopolitical religious US context in order to invite you to reflect on them in your own. Whereas Kassian has bemoaned the success of feminism as against G*d's biblical design of womanhood, manhood, and family, Nancy Cohen sees the developments of the last fifty years in the United States as the outcome of the conservative reaction against the sexual revolution of the 1960s. After the first birth-control pill went onto the market in 1960, it became possible for wo/men to claim their full citizen rights and better determine their future by being able to regulate conception and pregnancy.

The sexual fundamentalists, as Cohen calls the antifeminist movements, are fighting for the myth of the traditional middle-class,

---

[46] Ibid., 286–87. See also Carolyn McCulley, *Radical Womanhood: Feminine Faith in a Feminist World* (Chicago: Moody, 2008), which was written "by a former feminist who now finds herself embracing the distinction between men and women" (book jacket).

male-headed, white family of midcentury America, where man was the breadwinner and wo/man was the homemaker subject to many pregnancies, an ideal that "in previous eras only the urban, educated, Protestant upper class could afford to live by."[47] While in the twenty years after World War II white working-class men's families could live this ideal, black, immigrant, or poor families never could do so. By the late 1970s when income growth stagnated, even middle-class white married wo/men had to join the workforce in order to maintain the family income. Taking class and race analysis into account, Roman Catholic as well as Protestant attempts to the*logize the nuclear middle- to upper-class bourgeois family as ontologically given or divinely revealed is exposed as colonial elite male rhetoric promulgating the ethos of the White Lady and a defense of the kyriarchal order.[48]

Since they could not maintain this kyriarchal order, the Roman Catholic hierarchy and Protestant fundamentalist groups in the United States have resorted to political means for undoing the legal and ideological feminist gains of the last fifty years or so. Their politics are sanctioning and justifying the increasingly escalating "war" on all, but especially on poor and working-class wo/men. Their attacks on same-sex marriage and wo/men's reproductive rights to contraception and safe legal abortion on state and national levels are fought in the name of religious freedom. In this process, the rights of all wo/men are jeopardized.

One can shed more light on the Christian feminist right-wing countermovement when one looks at their arguments and politics in light of Marxist philosopher Louis Althusser's notion of "ideological interpellation." Althusser's account of "how a human being becomes a self-conscious subject" is part of his theoretical "argument that regimes or states are able to maintain control by reproducing subjects who believe that their position within the social structure is a natural

---

[47] Nancy L. Cohen, *Delirium: How the Sexual Counterrevolution Is Polarizing America: A Groundbreaking Investigation into the Shadow Movement that Fuels Our Political Wars* (Berkeley, CA: Counterpoint, 2012), 13.

[48] See Rosemary Radford Ruether, *Christianity and the Making of the Modern Family* (Boston: Beacon, 2000), 152–80.

one." Institutions such as schools, family, church, and/or the media provide the developing subject with categories in which she can recognize herself. Inasmuch as a person does so and embraces the practices associated with those institutions, she has been successfully "hailed" or "interpellated" and recognized herself as that subject who does those kind of things.[49]

By reinforcing the ideology of middle- and/or upper-class femininity, the New Feminism and True Woman movements thus bolster the kyriarchal subjectification of wo/men by proclaiming it as essential, natural, and revealed. Whereas the dominant ideology constantly works to seal the "cracks" generated by the contradictions of kyriarchal societies and religions, the feminist critique of kyriarchy points to contradictions between the democratic political promise of equality, self-determination, and freedom in modern societies as well as to wo/men's subordination, global exploitation, and exclusion in many areas of sociopolitical and religious life.[50]

In short, the "[anti]feminist" Religious Right seeks to strengthen kyriarchal capitalist power by resorting to essentialist scriptural or philosophical arguments and by organizing upper- and middle-class white wo/men against poor wo/men's exercise of their citizenship rights in society and church. To fully understand this political strategy, gender analysis does not suffice. What is necessary, as I have argued here, is to adopt a critical, intersectional-kyriarchal, the*logical analysis that can lift into consciousness how religious texts and doctrines inscribe kyriarchy and how kyriarchy reinscribes itself repeatedly into religious teaching and individual imagination.[51]

Moreover, the Religious Right has successfully organized grassroots wo/men into study and social movement groups to bolster

---

[49] See William Lewis, "Louis Althusser," in *The Stanford Encyclopedia of Philosophy*, ed. Edward N. Zalta, Winter 2009, http://plato.stanford.edu/archives/win2009/entries/althusser/.

[50] See Rosemary Hennessy, *Materialist Feminism and the Politics of Discourse* (New York: Routledge, 1993), 92.

[51] For a fuller development of this argument, see Elisabeth Schüssler Fiorenza, *The Power of the Word: Scripture and the Rhetoric of Empire* (Minneapolis, MN: Fortress, 2007), and Elisabeth Schüssler Fiorenza, *Democratizing Biblical Studies: Toward an Emancipatory Educational Space* (Louisville, KY: Westminster John Knox Press, 2009).

global "feminine" identity formation and religious authority dependence, whereas liberationist feminists have mostly organized in academic circles along the lines of cultural "identity politics" but are less
and less involved in providing an intellectual home to feminist grassroots movements in religion. This has been partly the case because
feminists in the*logy and feminist studies in religion have lacked the
institutional resources open to the New Feminism and True Woman
movements and have been little-recognized by so-called "secular" academic and movement feminists. However, in the face of the Right's
mobilization of wo/men, it is important that feminist liberationists
organize "consciousness-raising" or conscientization groups compelled by the following insight from bell hooks: Before we can change
kyriarchy as a system of interstructured dominations, "we have to
change ourselves and raise our own women's consciousness."[52]

hooks has pointed out that the radical movement politics of
wo/men's studies was replaced, in many cases, by the late 1970s with
liberal classroom reformism that replaced "the free for all" consciousness-raising groups. Once "women's studies replaced the consciousness-raising group as the primary site for feminist thinking and
strategies for social change, the movement lost its mass-based potential."[53] My own experience was similar. In the late 1970s, I was part of
a group of Catholic feminist the*logians who gathered to discuss feminist the*logical education. As far as I remember, we worked out several
different models of the*logical education, but I can only recall two of
them. The first was the central "school model" of the*logical education
that requires students to move to and have residence at a university or
the*logical school. This model was adopted and was institutionalized
as the ecumenical Women's Theological Center, which was located at
the Episcopal Divinity School in Cambridge, Massachusetts.

The other model proposed by the group in which I participated
was a decentered "satellite" model of the*logical education often

[52] See bell hooks, *Feminism Is for Everybody: Passionate Politics* (Cambridge, MA: South
End, 2000), 1–18.
[53] Ibid., 10.

used in D. Min. programs. Our educational model, however, would not orbit around a "school" but be resourced by a circle of feminist the*logians and movement workers. This model had as a goal to the*logically equip feminist leaders for forming feminist discussion/consciousness-raising groups of wo/men across the country. This model envisioned the*logical "leaders" (students) to stay in their "home spaces," to form local reading/discussion groups of wo/men as part of the program, and to meet several times a year regionally with a facilitating ("faculty") team of feminist the*logians. Our hope was that it would develop such strength that we also could meet annually or biannually for national and international feminist the*logical gatherings.

This model had several strengths: It did not require wo/men to move to a the*logical school and could enable especially married and financially limited wo/men to engage in feminist the*logical studies. At the same time, this model of the*logical education was designed to build up local feminist movement groups in parishes, neighborhoods, professional, family, or friendship circles, and put them in communication with each other about their faith and church. Thus, this model would simultaneously develop feminist the*logical leadership/the*logical education and facilitate wo/men's groups. However, the group didn't pursue this educational model at the time, and as far as I can see, it has not been developed and realized in another the*logical context.

As a consequence, feminist the*logy and studies in religion have been, for the most part, developed by the second and third generation of feminist the*logians in an academic context and around academic organizations. The book *Frontiers in Catholic Feminist Theology: Shoulder to Shoulder*, edited by Susan Abraham and Elena Procario-Foley, may serve as an example.[54] The editors state: "This book has its origins in the Workgroup for Constructive Theology" and that it seeks to bring together Catholic feminist the*logizing and teaching in terms of

---

54 Susan Abraham and Elena Procario-Foley, eds., *Frontiers in Catholic Feminist Theology: Shoulder to Shoulder* (Minneapolis, MN: Fortress, 2009).

the*logical education in Catholic colleges. However, such a location of feminist the*logy and the*logical education in the academy has had the tendency to make feminist the*logy primarily accountable to the academy, which institutionally marginalizes it, co-opts its frameworks, or altogether silences feminist the*logical work. Feminist the*logians in Catholic institutions are increasingly controlled by the hierarchy, and if they are nuns, wo/men are subject to repression and silencing by the Vatican as the examples of Ivone Gebara from Brazil, Elizabeth Johnson at Fordham University, and Margaret Farley, the preeminent feminist Catholic ethicist who taught at Yale University.

In contrast to the situation of feminist academic the*logy, rightwing education of wo/men in the doctrines of the New Feminism has garnered great institutional support. Thus, the the*logical feminist "conscientization" model that we envisioned but did not realize more than thirty years ago has been co-opted and partially actualized, for instance, by ENDOW (Educating on the Nature and Dignity of Women), albeit with a different content. ENDOW was created by Terri Polakovic, who in November 2011 received for her work the Pro Ecclesia et Pontifice Cross, the highest papal honors a layperson can receive. According to her, ENDOW was active in more than eighty dioceses in 2011 and has organized and involved almost 3,800 wo/men in ENDOW study groups. Many more undoubtedly access their attractive website. She explains:

> ENDOW stands for Educating on the Nature and Dignity of Women. What we do is develop study guides for women to use in small study groups. All women start out reading John Paul II's 1988 *"Letter to Women."* Most women have never read a Church document. We think this is a great place to start. We have 10 additional studies, as well… The high-school girls totally got it, but when they went home, some of their mothers rejected what we were teaching. That's when we realized that we need to teach the mothers, so that they could form their daughter. This year we're focusing more on the middle-school and high-school programs. There's a great need to reach girls younger and younger in our culture.[55]

I completely agree with Polakovic's last sentence, "that there is a great need" to reach and teach girls: Feminists in religion need to create spaces for feminist religious education of girls and boys because there is a great need for it in the context of ever-increasing global exploitation of wo/men. The most pressing questions to address for feminist studies, in general, and feminist studies in religion, the*logians, teachers, and ministers, in particular, are not only "How can we create alternative feminist organizations, groups, and media for *conscientization* and support in the*logy and religious communities locally and globally?" but also "How can we unmask the New Feminism as a kyriarchal theory serving global neoliberal exploitation?" Throughout the centuries, malestream theology and institutions of higher learning have silenced wo/men, barred us from religious positions of authority, and excluded us from ordained ministry and academic the*logy. Hence, feminist the*logy specifically has to empower wo/men for becoming the*logical subjects, for participating in the critical construction of religious-the*logical meanings, and for claiming our authority to do so. After centuries of silencing and exclusion from the*logical studies and religious leadership, Christian wo/men today have moved into academy and ministry to claim our religious heritage and agency. In the past forty years, we wo/men in religion have reclaimed our voice and have begun to speak.

Rather than put down such insistence on the importance of feminist theory, the*logy, heritance, and the need for feminist the*logical education as too intellectual and too academic, we need to spend time asking: How do we create religious institutional spaces that can sustain alternative feminist liberationist movements in times of neoliberal globalization? How can we create radical democratic *ekklēsia* spaces for articulating, developing, communicating, and

---

55 A Google search for "New Feminism" turned up the following article: Tim Drake, "Teaching John Paul II's 'New Feminism'—1 Woman at a Time," March 10, 2011, http://www.ncregister.com/daily-news/teaching-john-paul-iis-new-feminism-1-woman-at-a-time#ixzz1zlCq6ZJT.

debating feminist theories, the*logies, and spiritual practices of con-scientization? How can we develop a sociopolitical imaginary as the alternative to kyriarchy that opens up a different feminist future?

I attempt to wrestle with the last question in the next chapter by developing the notion of the *kosmopolis of wo/men* as a sociopolitical-religious imaginary that seeks to articulate creative and symbolic dimensions of a sociopolitical-religious world, where human beings create their ways of living together and representing that collective life.[56]

---

[56] John B. Thompson, *Studies in the Theory of Ideology* (Cambridge: Polity, 1984), 6.

CHAPTER 3

Toward the Ekklēsia and Kosmopolis of Wo/men

Feminists in religion have reacted against the essentializing "gospel of femininity" with either/or options such as "either religious or feminist," and "either fight for equal rights of wo/men to be clergymen or move out of religion and religious institutions such as the church, synagogue, mosque, or temple." Feminist "either/or" options require either assent to kyriarchal religion or eschewal of the spiritual resources of religion in wo/men's struggles for surviving global exploitation. Such either/or options are usually formulated in terms of the other. However, as I have outlined earlier in this book, feminists in religion must reject such either/or options and come together in the struggle against kyriarchal domination, and this coming together is often referred to as "solidarity" or "friendship."

Right-wing Christian religion preaches an essentialist feminine subordinate identity formation modeled after the cultural ideal of the White Lady and promises a world of subordination as "good news" for wo/men. This "gospel of femininity" is kyriarchal because it advocates the second-class citizenship of wo/men in religious terms. It also supports capitalist "globalization from above," which has resulted in the denial of human rights to wo/men and the increase in poverty among wo/men and children dependent on wo/men.

By inculcating essentialized feminine identity as subordinated identity, the "gospel of femininity" serves the interests of those who promote global exploitation and seek to cut or eliminate the social welfare net that makes survival possible for poor and disadvantaged wo/men and their children.[1] By organizing wo/men in religion on the ideological grounds of "the eternal feminine," or the "feminine genius," this "gospel of femininity" attempts to defend the privileges of white middle- and upper-class wo/men who, until the globalization of markets, had the privilege of not having to work outside the home. Whereas the rhetoric of gender essentialism and male/female gender dualism of right-wing feminism has glossed over differences among wo/men, global liberationist feminism in religion has celebrated differences between and among wo/men. However, we have not been able to organize and mobilize wo/men in religion across religious, cultural, and national differences into a transnational alliance of a global feminist movement in religion. If we want to come together in the struggle against kyriarchal domination, feminists need to reject such either/or options.

For such a coming together, I have proposed the imagery—that is, the formation of mental images, figures, or likenesses—of the *ekklēsia* of wo/men and more recently also that of the *kosmopolis of wo/men*. I have done so, although I fully realize both are notions that have been used and misused for Western hegemonic interests. In order to distance them from neoliberal global meanings I have retained their Greek spelling to indicate their initial meanings. Moreover, I have taken these words out of their original masculine-determined context and placed them in a critical feminist framework. Finally, in today's world of global media and "global citizens" rhetoric, such a "working together must be envisioned in political terms and aspirations everyone."[2]

---

[1] For a problematizing comparison of the difference between indigenous notions of duality and complementarity in indigenous spirituality with the notion of complementarity in Roman Catholic the*logy, see Sylvia Marcos, "Indigenous Spirituality and the Politics of Justice: Voices from the First Summit of Indigenous Women of the Americas," in *Women and Indigenous Religions*, ed. Sylvia Marcos (Santa Barbara, CA: Praeger, 2010), 45–68. For a critical assessment, see Morna Macleod, "Drawing the Connection: Mayan Women's Quest for a Gendered Spirituality," in Marcos, *Women and Indigenous Religions*, 195–215.

[2] Global Citizen, https://www.globalcitizen.org.

Whereas the term *ekklēsia* has Christian connotations, the notion of *cosmopolis/cosmopolitan* has emerged anew in the context of neoliberal globalization. Although the term has mostly lost its Christian accent, it has still Christian eschatological overtones that need to be scrutinized with a hermeneutics of suspicion. Classic Greek philosophy did not favor cosmopolitanism derived from the Greek word *kosmopolitēs*, or citizen of the world, because one's obligation was not primarily to the whole world but rather to one's particular *polis* and polity. In the first centuries CE, the Stoics understood the entire *kosmos* as a *polis*, but they argued that one needed to limit one's political engagement to one's *polis* since it was impossible to serve as a citizen of the whole world.

Early Christians took up this Stoic notion of two cities (the world/cosmos and the local city), the cosmopolis and the polis, and understood it as G*d's *polis of love* and one's native human polity. Augustine, for example, understood it as both the earthly polity characterized by love of Self and the city of G*d as belonging to those who love G*d. In so doing, one became a "fellow citizen with the saints" (Eph 2:20). However, these two cities were not separate but intertwined until the last judgment.

Today, there also exists a wide variety in contemporary philosophy of cosmopolitanism. Political, economic, and moral cosmopolitanisms are widely discussed. However, no one seems to envision and argue for a uniform world-state. Most debated is economic cosmopolitanism, or neoliberal capitalism, which has produced vast inequalities of extreme wealth and global poverty, large-scale migration, and the lack of living wage jobs for all the world's citizens.[3] These developments have especially hit hard the wo/men and children of the world who are dependent on wo/men. Hence, a cosmopolitan feminism "rejects the Western-centric, falsely universalized, and undemocratic imposition of narrowly defined understandings of human rights" but it retains "a commitment to democratically grounded, emancipatory political projects."[4]

---

[3] This summary account is based on Pauline Kleingeld and Eric Brown, "Cosmopolitanism," *Stanford Encyclopedia of Philosophy*, 2014, htpp://plato.stanford.edu/entries/cosmopolitanism.

[4] Niamh Reilly, "Cosmopolitan Feminism and Human Rights," *Hypatia* 22, no. 4 (2007):180–98, quotation on 181.

In the face of current neoliberal global situations of poverty, migration, environmental destruction, or grave violations of basic human rights, I argue, feminists in religion need to develop cosmopolitan feminist the*logies and religious visions. As Korean the*logian Namsoon Kang forcefully states:

> The new context of globalization points to the mandate for a new approach to feminist theological issues and concerns, an approach based on a recognition of fundamental mutuality and interconnectivity of nations and regions, and a desire for transnational, transregional, and transethnic cooperation, alliances and solidarities, rather than the balkanization or theological tribalism of feminist theological discourse and issues based on national, cultural, regional, or ethnic divide.[5]

Ekklesia of Wo/men Struggling for the "Democracy to Come" (Derrida)

In a December 1997 discussion on Politics and Friendship at the University of Sussex's Centre for Modern French Thought, philosopher Jacques Derrida pointed out that in his more recent work he had tried alongside others "to rethink what the political is, what is involved precisely in the dissemination of the political field," since friendship had not been considered a political concept, although friendship "plays an organizing role in the definition of justice, of democracy even." Since in the texts of Plato and Aristotle, elite male "friendship is defined as the essential virtue,"[6] Derrida deconstructed this conceptualization of Greek and modern democracy based on notions of brotherhood and male friendship, which exclude political

---

[5] Kang, *Diasporic Feminist Theology*, 252.
[6] Geoffrey Bennington and Jacques Derrida, "Politics and Friendship: A Discussion with Jacques Derrida," December 1, 1997, http://www.livingphilosophy.org/Derrida-politics-friendship.htm.

friendship between men and wo/men as well as between wo/men and wo/men. The prevailing model of friendship and of democracy is thus rooted in fraternity-brotherhood.

Kyriarchal Democracy and Friendship

Just as in the political delineation of kyriarchal democracy, philosophical discussions of friendship in the West are based on Aristotle. Aristotle recognized three bases or types of friendship: One might like someone because they are good, because they are useful, or because they are pleasant. When Aristotle began his discussion of friendship, he introduced a notion of friendship that philosopher Richard Kraut sees as central to Aristotle's understanding of friendship: A *genuine friend* is someone who loves or likes another person for the sake of that other person.[7] Wanting what is good for the sake of another Aristotle called "good will" (*eunoia*) and friendship (*philia*). Good will is reciprocal, provided that each recognizes the presence of this attitude in the other. It seems that Aristotle was leaving room for the idea that in all three kinds of friendships (goodness, pleasure, and advantage, and even those based on advantage and pleasure alone), the individuals wish each other well for the sake of the other. But Aristotle did not develop this possibility. Rather, he emphasized that it is in friendships based on character that one finds a desire to benefit the other person for the sake of the other person. He stated, "Those who wish good things to their friends for the sake of the latter are friends most of all, because they do so because of their friends themselves, and not coincidentally."[8] And also, "When one benefits someone not because of the kind of person s/he is, but only because of the advantages to oneself, then, one is not a friend

---

[7] In the following elaboration, I follow Richard Kraut's interpretation of Aristotle's *Nicomachean Ethics*. See Richard Kraut, "Aristotle's Ethics," in *Stanford Encyclopedia of Philosophy*, May 1, 2001, rev. April 21, 2014, http://plato.stanford.edu/entries/aristotle-ethics/.

[8] Aristotle, *Nichomachean Ethics*, 1156b9–11. Aristotle, *The Nicomachean Ethics: Oxford World Classics*, trans. David Ross, Introduction by Lesley Brown (New York: Oxford University Press, 2009).

towards the other person, but only towards the profit that comes one's way."[9]

According to Aristotle, friendships based on character are the ones in which each (lord)-person benefits the other for the sake of the other (elite male), and these are the truest friendships of all. Because each party benefits the other, forming such friendships is advantageous. And since each enjoys the trust and companionship of the other, there is considerable pleasure in these relationships as well. Because these perfect (elite male) friendships produce advantages and pleasures for each of the parties, there is some basis for going along with common usage and calling any relationship entered into for the sake of just one of these goods a "friendship."

However, friendships based on advantage or pleasure alone deserve also to be called friendships because in full-fledged friendships these two properties, advantage and pleasure, are present. It is striking that in the *Nicomachean Ethics*, Aristotle never said that the uniting factor in all friendships is the desire each friend has for the good of the other. But there is no reason why acts of friendship should not be undertaken partly for the good of one's friend and partly for one's own good. Acting for the sake of another does not in itself demand self-sacrifice. It requires caring about someone other than oneself, but it does not demand some loss of care for oneself. For when we know how to benefit a friend for her sake, we exercise ethical virtues, and this is precisely what our happiness consists in.

Rethinking Kyriarchal Democracy in Terms of Friendship

Hence, we need to rethink democracy beyond the classical political model, which is phallocentric and male-centered, Derrida argued, and we must rearticulate it with a different concept of friendship. Since there is inequality and repression in the traditional concept of friendship, we have to displace it in the name of democracy—a

---

[9] Ibid., 1157a15–16.

"democracy to come." By "democracy to come" Derrida did not mean a new regime, a new organization of nation states, or a future democracy. Rather, this "democracy we dream of is linked in its concept to a promise," which has inscribed equality, freedom of speech, and freedom of the press—"all these things are inscribed as promises within democracy." However, "to come" does not mean just a future democracy. Rather, "we have to do right here and now what has to be done for it." If we separate democracy from the name of a regime, a governmental institutional form, "we then can give this name 'democracy' to any kind of experience in which there is equality, justice, equity, respect for the singularity of the Other at work, so to speak—then it's democracy here and now; but of course this implies that we do not confine democracy to the political, in the classic sense, or to the nation-state or to citizenship."[10]

Such an understanding of the promise of democracy requires the urgent "transformation of the concept of the political, of the concept of democracy, and of the concept of friendship." According to Derrida, it requires hospitality—the unconditional welcoming of the other, whoever he or she is. This concept of hospitality calls for "a new concept of democracy grounded—assuming this is a ground, and I am not sure it is—grounded on this groundless experience of friendship, which shouldn't be limited in the way it has been, and a concept of democracy which would redefine the political not only beyond the nation state, but beyond the cosmopolitical itself."[11]

Democracy and Brotherhood

Such a new concept of democracy, of the "democracy to come," which is "grounded in the groundless experience of friendship," needs to give special feminist attention to two obstacles that keep "fraternal" friendship and democracy in place: the sameness of friendship and the culture of neoliberalism. In her discussion of "Aristotle

---

[10] Ibid.
[11] Ibid.

and Derrida on Friendship," feminist philosopher Sandra Lynch pointed out that Aristotle characterized the friend as another self and stressed the notion of congeneric or sibling friendship to ensure that genuine or true friendship could not be defined in utilitarian terms.[12] However, defining friendship in terms of brotherhood or even sib-linghood does not allow for difference but requires sameness and commitment to sameness. Hence, the notion of sisterhood as an orga-nizing metaphor for the wo/men's liberation movement has been rightly criticized for disregarding kyriarchal differences among wo/men and has led to the critique of the identity category "woman." Ideal friendship defined as "friendship between women" also repro-duces the culture of sameness rather than a commitment to recogniz-ing and changing kyriarchal differences and subordinations.

Moreover, Aristotle idealized friendship between good men as the basis for political concord and democracy. He regarded the Greek *polis* as an arena of like-minded men related in citizenship by the bonds of friendship, stating, "These men agree about their interests, adopt the same policy, and put their common resolves into effect."[13] The notion of citizens as "friends and brothers" or as "friends and sis-ters" suggests not only equality of rights but also familial intimacy. This idealization of friendship, according to Lynch, distorts any con-sideration of *philia*/friendship in terms of intimacy and emotional attachment, on the one hand, and denies the possibility of conflict within the *polis* arising from potentially rival conceptions of the good, or the other.[14]

The idealization of citizens as friends and of friends as "second selves" totalizes friendship and makes it an impossible ideal. This emphasis on congeniality implies equality that is understood as sameness. It does not take into account structural differences and kyr-iarchal subordinations. It does not have the power to transform divi-sions and subjugations into genuine differences. Deep friendship

---

[12] Sandra Lynch, "Aristotle and Friendship," *Contretemps* 3 (July 2002): 98–108.

[13] Aristotle, *Nicomachean Ethics*, Book 9, 1168a18–b64.

[14] Lynch, "Aristotle and Friendship," 101.

with the other is only possible in common struggles for change and transformation; it is only possible in the "democracy to come" in and through our struggles for equality in difference. In short, we need to stop thinking and acting in terms of congeniality, sameness, and otherness and instead start thinking in terms of friendship that is actionable only in a space of equality among different visions and positions.

Friendship, Democracy, and the Culture of Neoliberalism

A present totalizing form of kyriarchy is the culture and economics of neoliberalism that has co-opted Aristotle's second and third elements of friendship, that of use and that of delight and pleasure. Whereas "true friendship" is restricted to male equals, that is, to the *kyrioi* in the city-state, friendship of use and friendship of delight do not necessarily require such equality and can be mobilized in kyriarchal structures and for kyriocentric ends.

In his book *Friendship in an Age of Economics*, political philosopher Todd May argues that neoliberalism is not only a theory of market relations but also a theory of human relations.[15] We are encouraged to think not only of our work but also of our lives in economic terms, and friendship is no exception. Aristotle's friendship of desire is lived out in such a society by the figure of the consumer, and friendship of use is enacted in and through entrepreneurship. We all participate in these two forms of friendship in global neoliberal societies. Like Derrida, May recognizes xenophobic reactions against displaced populations and strangers, the threat of global warming, political polarization, unemployment, poverty, and centuries of exploitation as well as the devaluation of social equality and democratic multiplicity as a product of our

---

[15] Todd May, *Friendship in an Age of Economics: Resisting the Force of Neoliberalism* (Lanham, MD: Lexington, 2012). See also Melanie Gross and Gabriele Winkler, eds., *Queer-, Feministische Kritiken neoliberaler Verhältnisse* (Münster: Unrast, 2007).

times, the product of neoliberalism. He defines neoliberalism as the view "that an unfettered (or largely unfettered) capitalist market is the best and most efficient way for an economy to be run."[16]

Hence, the theory of neoliberalism was better suited for a globalized market than Keynesian theory, which argued that governments must step in and intervene in the market during times when people are too poor or afraid to spend money. Neoliberalism in contrast "holds that, rather than relying on the government to ensure the welfare of its citizens, a country must instead rely on the mechanisms of a capitalist market."[17] This shift in economics, which has increased the numbers of the poor around the globe and has rendered them much more vulnerable, is a shift from a social democracy or "welfare" society to a neoliberal one. In such a neoliberal world, not only friendship but also feminist organization is in danger of becoming a practice of consumption and investment.

May goes on to argue that true or deep friendship can be articulated as an antidote to neoliberalism insofar as it cultivates "the kinds of people that can recognize and respect others even when they disagree with them. . . . It does so through the mechanism of trust. . . . I can only be in solidarity with those I trust. Friendship trains me in that trust, and in doing so, trains me to interact with others in a common project even where I disagree with them."[18]

May concedes that deep friendship can become self-enclosed and inimical to political solidarity. Nevertheless, "those who have learned to cultivate close friendships are more rather than less likely to be able to immerse themselves in movements that require a solid, if not intimate, bond among participants."[19] He recognizes that "deep friendships" tend more to "one-to-one friendships," which are by their very nature restricted to a few friendships with people of the same race, class, or sex/gender. Such deep, one-on-one friendships "contrast with the requirements of political solidarity." Nevertheless,

---

[16] May, *Friendship*, 4.
[17] Ibid.
[18] Ibid., 137.
[19] Ibid., 140.

he maintains, "there are aspects of friendship that can lead one toward political involvement . . . one that is oriented toward a political solidarity in resistance to neoliberalism."[20]

However, for "hospitality" (Derrida) or "deep friendship" (May) to be realized, I would argue that it must be situated in the everyday struggles of wo/men against kyriarchal dehumanization that are inspired by the vision of the "democracy to come." True or deep friendship is to be situated in and oriented toward the commitment and struggles to change kyriarchal relations of domination if it should not foster neoliberal mind-sets of exploitation. Only "friendship in struggles for change and transformation" can be "deep friendship." In order to recognize such movements in the space of religion, in general, and Christianity, in particular, I have suggested that we understand and name "the *ekklēsia of wo/men*" as such a global justice movement for the "democracy to come" that is inspired by "friendship in struggle."

The *Kosmopolis of Wo/men*: Envisioning the "World to Come"

Since the notion of the *ekklēsia of wo/men* can easily be misunderstood in terms of either liberal democracy or Christian church, I want to place it in the political frame of the *kosmopolis of wo/men* but will retain the Greek writing *ekklēsia* in order not to be further misunderstood in terms of liberal cosmopolitanism. The term *kosmopolitēs* means "citizen of the world" and has its roots in classical Greek philosophy. It was taken up by early Christians and canonized by Augustine in his conceptualization of two cities: the city of G*d and the universal but inferior earthly city.[21] However, our contemporary understanding of *cosmos* does not just mean world but also the universe. In light of neoliberal globalization, it is important to mark this difference and understand it also in terms of ecological citizenship.[22]

---

[20] Ibid., 126–27.
[21] Pauline Klengeld, "Cosmopolitanism," *Stanford Encyclopedia of Philosophy*, http://plato.stanford.edu/entries/cosmopolitanism/.
[22] See Angel Valencia Sáiz, "Globalization, Cosmopolitanism, and Ecological Citizenship," *Environmental Politics* 14, no. 2 (2005): 163–78.

We must not overlook, however, that the radical democratic practices of the *ekklēsia of wo/men* need to remain oriented toward the wider
kosmopolis of wo/men and take responsibility for its well-being. To avoid
narrowing the meaning of *ekklēsia* to church and to safeguard its political
radical democratic understanding, it needs to be conjoined with the *kosmopolis*, an aggregate of the Greek words *kosmos* (world/universe) and
polis (city-state), from which the much-controverted idea of cosmopolitanism derives.[23] However, as we saw with Derrida, the "democracy to
come" must go beyond the cosmopolitical in the traditional sense and
must be rooted in a different vision of friendship and hospitality, a hospitality that "should be neither assimilation, acculturation, nor simply
the occupation of my space by the other."[24] Rather, hospitality is a very
general name for all our relations to the other and needs to be reinvented
at every second because it is something "without a pre-given rule."[25]

According to fourth-century BCE Greek philosopher Diogenes
Laertius, a cosmopolitan is "a citizen of the cosmos." Contemporary
German philosopher Thomas Pogge identified the following three
elements shared by different cosmopolitan articulations:

- The ultimate units of concern are *human beings or persons*
  rather than collectives such as families, tribes, ethnic or religious communities, or nations.
- *Universality* insofar as ultimate concern pertains to every
  human being equally and not merely to some subset such as
  men, rich people, Jews, or white men.
- *Generality*: Persons are units of concern for everyone, not just
  for their related compatriots or members of their religious
  community. Their special status has global force.[26]

---

[23] For a short history of cosmopolitanism, see Seyla Benhabib, *Dignity in Adversity:
Human Rights in Troubled Times* (Cambridge: Polity, 2011), 3–19; and K. Anthony
Appiah, *Cosmopolitanism: Ethics in a World of Strangers* (New York: W. W. Norton and
Co., 2006).
[24] Bennington and Derrida, "Politics and Friendship."
[25] Ibid.
[26] Thomas Pogge, "Cosmopolitanism and Sovereignty," in *World Poverty and Human
Rights: Cosmopolitan Responsibilities and Reforms* (Cambridge: Polity, 2002), 168–95,
quotation on 169.

However, such an articulation of cosmopolitanism in individual personal terms occludes the cosmological vision evoked by the word *kosmos*, which means "the world" or "universe." This cosmological accent stresses the responsibility that humans have as part of the cosmic web of life for the care of the planet and its well-being. Ecofeminism makes the connection that the oppression of wo/men and of people of color in a system controlled by ruling-class males and the devastation of the planet are two forms of violence that reinforce and feed upon each other.[27]

According to Niamh Reilly, cosmopolitan feminism entails the following mutually constitutive elements that "need to be taken together to understand cosmopolitan feminism as a transformative political framework."[28] This framework needs to be further adjusted to that of feminist cosmopolitanism in religion. Building on her statement, I would like to point out the following elements of such a feminist cosmopolitan framework:

- Critical engagement with public international law complemented with a discussion of religious law and belief-systems;
- A global feminist consciousness and spirituality that challenges the systemic interplay of kyriarchal power relations in society and religion;
- Recognition of kyriarchal intersectionality and an organized commitment to cross-boundaries, transcultural and religious dialogue, networking, and social-the*logical political criticism;
- Development of regional and global collaborative advocacy strategies and intellectual exchange around concrete issues and struggles;
- Utilization of existing institutions and the creation of new forms of communication, local intercultural groups, global

---

[27] Mary Judith Ress, *Ecofeminism in Latin America* (Maryknoll, NY: Orbis, 2006), 110; see also Rosemary Radford Ruether, *Women Healing the Earth: Third World Women on Ecology, Feminism, and Religion* (Maryknoll, NY: Orbis, 1996); and Ivone Gebara, *Longing for Running Water: Ecofeminism and Liberation* (Minneapolis, MN: Fortress, 1999).
[28] Reilly, "Cosmopolitan Feminism and Human Rights," 184.

transnational organizations, and global forums as sites of cosmopolitan exchange between feminists in and outside religions, transreligion or interreligious solidarity, and
cosmopolitan citizenship.[29]

The *kosmopolis* is the imaginary site of the *ekklēsia of wo/men*,
where wo/men citizens gather for feminist religious "world making"
for the "democracy to come." These religious-political practices of
world making in the *ekklēsia of wo/men* as the decision-making assembly of the *kosmopolis* have to be governed by the egalitarian values and
visions of justice and well-being for everyone without exception.
According to the theoretical vision, but not the historical realization,
of democracy, all those living in the *kosmopolis* should have equal status as world citizens and be able to decide their and their children's
future. In theory, all citizens of the *kosmopolis* are created equal in
rights, speech, and power—they are created in the Divine image.

I have introduced and explicated in this work the imaginary of
the *ekklēsia of wo/men* as a key radical democratic, theoretical, and
practical political site of such a cosmopolitan feminism. Adding the
marker "wo/men," which signifies all those excluded from democracy
to the democratic concepts *ekklēsia* and *kosmopolis*, cautions readers
not to identify democracy with hegemonic US democracy, which,
according to First Nations feminist scholar Andrea Smith, is articulating "itself as a democratic country, on one hand, and simultaneously
founding itself on the past and current genocide of Native peoples, on
the other hand."[30]

---

[29] On the feminist discussion of citizenship, see Patricia Durish, *Citizenship and Difference: Feminist Debates*, Annotated Bibliographies Series of the Transformative Learning Centre (Toronto: Ontario Institute for Studies in Education, 2002); Monika
Mookherjee, "Affective Citizenship: Feminism, Postcolonialism, and the Politics of
Recognition," *Critical Review of International Social and Political Philosophy* 8, no. 1
(2005): 31–50; and Baukje Prins, "Mothers and Muslims, Sisters and Sojourners: The
Contested Boundaries of Feminist Citizenship," in *Handbook of Gender and Women's
Studies*, eds. Kathy Davis, Mary Evans, and Judith Lorber (London: Sage, 2006),
234–50.
[30] Andrea Smith, "First Nation, Empire, and Globalization," in Fulkerson and Briggs,
Oxford Handbook of Feminist Theology, 307–31, quotation on 314–15.

By introducing the radical democratic notions of the *kosmopolis* and *ekklēsia of wo/men* as an alternative religious-political feminist vision and option to that of essentialist and essentializing femininity discourses, I seek to elaborate the *ekklēsia of wo/men* as the decision-making congress of the *kosmopolis of wo/men* and to also reject the dualistic division between religion and culture, religion and democratic rights, or religious and secular wo/men's movements. Such a reframing is possible because the Greek word *ekklēsia* has a double meaning: It connotes both the democratic assembly of full citizens and the religious community.

The *Ekklēsia* of the *Kosmopolis of Wo/men*

The *ekklēsia of wo/men* is then best envisioned in light of cosmopolitan ecofeminist theory as the decision-making democratic assembly of all the inhabitants of the *kosmos*—humans, animals, plants, or stars. It is an imaginary that seeks to create the connection between the local/particular struggles of wo/men and the vision of a *kosmopolis*, a global society and religion of justice and well-being that no longer can be imagined without wo/men citizens.

The Ekklēsia/Congress of Wo/men

As I have explained previously, the Greek word *ekklēsia* does not mean in the first place "church" but rather a democratic assembly or congress that deliberates and decides the welfare of the city, nation, and world. As argued in the discussion above, it is rooted in Western political thought and needs to be translated in terms of other cultural traditions that develop similar visions. In a religious Christian context, it has been co-opted to mean "church" but it originally referred to the democratic meaning and structures of the Christian community.[31] The terms *synagogue* in Judaism and *ummah* in Islam can also

---

[31] For the democratic notion of *ekklēsia* in the Pauline letters, see Anna C. Miller, *Corinthian Democracy: Democratic Discourse in 1 Corinthians* (Eugene, OR: Pickwick, 2015).

have such democratic overtones. In short, the *ekklēsia of wo/men* as the *congress of wo/men* seeks to name the sociocultural and religious emancipatory movements of the "democracy to come." Polish feminist the*logian El bieta Adamiak has pointed to a recent historical example of how such a democratic vision of *ekklēsia* is being historically realized as the Congress of Women in Poland. The translation of *ekklēsia* as "congress" is apt in view of the political character of the event.

> The 6th Congress of Women took place on 9th and 10th May, 2014. It was a very special event because of two anniversaries that Poland was celebrating this year – 25 years after systemic transformation and 10 years after Polish accession to the European Union. The 6th Congress brought together over 9 thousand people (mostly women) from all over Poland. Foreign delegations from several other European countries also reached Warsaw. Representatives of Estonia, Lithuania, Latvia, Czech Republic, Germany, France, Finland, Norway, Sweden, Bulgaria but also United States and Tunisia managed to participate in our event. Even Indian feminists delegation attended the Congress. The 6th Congress of Women, under the banner of "community, equality, responsibility", was inaugurated by its originators and activists – Henryka Bochniarz, Magdalena Sroda and Dorota Warakomska.[32]

This congress acted not only in the interest of politics and society but also in the realm of religion by collectively drafting and sending a letter to Pope Francis. Moreover, the Congress acted in the interest of all wo/men, not only those living in Poland, and hence was correctly seen as an international Congress of Wo/men.

The qualification of *congress/ekklēsia* with the term *wo/men* does not just serve as a communicative tool for indicating how a diverse and multiform wo/men's movement may be imagined. It also seeks to

---

[32] "The 6th Congress of Women Has Ended," May 20, 2014, https://www.kongreskobiet.pl/en-EN/news/show/6th_congress_of_women_has_ended.

signify the multiple forms in which the *congress/ekklēsia of wo/men* is lived today in order to presage the rich diversity of the radical democratic *ekklēsia* of the future. Wo/men are not the same, nor do they have an essence in common that makes them different from men. There are as many differences between wo/men and within wo/men as there are between men and wo/men. Wo/men are not just determined by gender, but also by race, class, ethnicity, culture, age, sexual preference, and religion. Identity is not stable but changes over the course of time. Hence, the oxymoron *ekklēsia of wo/men* should not be understood in the cultural terms of femininity as promoting the ideal of the White Lady, but as modeling a multivocal feminist movement for wo/men's rights in society as well as religion and for change of both. Such feminist diversity of *ekklēsia* is actualized in worldwide wo/men's movements in religion and democratic feminist grassroots movements around the globe.

Thus, the *congress/ekklēsia of wo/men* understands itself as not just a movement to change church and religion, but sees its work as part and parcel of all social movements for changing relations of domination in societies and religions.[33] Yet, as French feminist Christine Delphy has so forcefully reminded us: "We do not know what the values, individual personality traits, and culture of a non-hierarchical society would be like and we have great difficulty in imagining it. But to imagine it we must think that it is possible. Practices produce values: other practices produce other values."[34]

As the assembly of the friends and prophets of Divine Wisdom, the cosmopolitan *ekklēsia of wo/men* in religion has to come together for envisioning and deliberating the best course of action in very concrete situations of struggle. Feminists in religion have to build global, transcultural, cosmopolitan organizations for articulating a wisdom

---

[33] Hedwig Meyer-Wilmes, "The Diversity of Ministry in a Postmodern Church," in *The Non-Ordination of Women and the Politics of Power*, eds. Elisabeth Schüssler Fiorenza and Hermann Häring (Maryknoll, NY: Orbis, 1999), 80.
[34] Christine Delphy, "Rethinking Sex and Gender," in Juschka, *Feminism in the Study of Religion*, 411–23, quotation on 422.

spirituality of cosmic world citizenship and for securing the welfare of everyone in the *kosmos/world* and of the *kosmos* itself. A radical democratic, political, and spiritual cosmopolitan practice is not supposed to be disengaged and detached. On the contrary, it is to enable people to be the arbiters of their fate and to promote the well-being of the earth.

The Kosmopolis of Wo/men

With the expression *kosmopolis of wo/men*, I have a heuristic construct in mind that is similar to what postcolonial feminist scholar Chandra Talpade Mohanty has called the "imagined community of Third World oppositional struggles."[35] She envisions it as the kind of space that provides a political rather than biological or cultural basis for alliance between wo/men of all colors and moves away from essentialist notions of third-world feminisms. Within the context of social movements for change, one can theorize the *ekklēsia of wo/men's* responsibility for the *kosmopolis* and all of creation not only as a virtual, utopian space but also as an already partially realized space of radical equality and friendship in struggle, as a site of feminist work for transforming social and religious kyriarchal institutions.

Emancipatory social movements, including the wo/men's liberation movements in religion, do not struggle for equal rights in order to become masculine and the same as elite men. They struggle in order to achieve the rights, benefits, and privileges of equal authority and citizenship that are legitimately ours but denied to us by the kyriarchal regimes of most societies and the major world religions. We respect particular struggles while at the same time forging complex solidarities in the global struggles against interlocking systems of domination. To quote Smith at length:

---

[35] Mohanty, "Under Western Eyes."

It is obvious that there are no clear pathways to liberation. . . . We make the way as we walk. [Grassroots movements] unleash their political imaginaries as they struggle for a liberation without guarantees. . . . They provide an alternative vision of globalization that is not structured through empire but through principles of mutual cooperation and social justice. The strategies of this kind of revolution are contextual, flexible, ever changing, and open to all possible alliances. To quote one Native wo/man activist, "you can't win a revolution on your own, and we are about nothing short of a revolution. Anything else is simply not worth our time."[36]

A Feminist Democratic Tradition: Anna Julia Cooper

However, when I first began to theorize the *ekklēsia* and *kosmopolis of wo/men* as an alternative imaginary and a mediating radical democratic concept, I was unaware that the American suffrage movement already had employed the symbol of democracy as a religious-biblical symbol in its struggle for justice. Womanist scholar Karen Baker-Fletcher pointed, for example, to African-American educator and suffragist Anna Julia Cooper, for whom, Baker-Fletcher argues, equality and freedom were not simply physical states but political-spiritual realities.[37] Cooper believed that democratic progress was "a shadow mark of the creator's image" derived "from the essential worth of humanity." Cooper envisioned a future for humanity that was governed by the principles of equality, freedom, and democracy, which were ontological universal aspects of human nature.[38]

Cooper understood democracy in religious terms and broadened the suffragist ethos of struggle for full citizenship when she insisted that democratic equality and freedom are G*d-given, inborn,

---

[36] Smith, "First Nation, Empire, and Globalization," 328–29.

[37] Karen Baker-Fletcher, *A Singing Something: Womanist Reflections on Anna Julia Cooper* (New York: Crossroad, 1994).

[38] Anna Julia Cooper, "Equality of Races and the Democratic Movement," privately printed pamphlet, Washington, DC, 1945, 5.

ontological capacities of every human being regardless of race, sex, class, and country. Against theories that claimed democracy, equality, and freedom as the property of the superior races of Western European civilization, Cooper insisted that these were inherent in the fact of being human and hence could never be suppressed.[39] While I conceive of the notion of the *ekklēsia of wo/men* quite differently and speak to a different rhetorical and historical context, it nevertheless is a part of and continues the radical democratic religious-feminist tradition Cooper envisioned.[40] This submerged feminist tradition of radical democratic religious agency and emancipatory biblical interpretation in which my own work is rooted has claimed and continues to claim the authority and right of wo/men to interpret experience, Bible, tradition, and religion from our own perspective and in our own interests.

This tradition has insisted that equality, freedom, and democracy cannot be realized if wo/men's voices are not raised, heard, and heeded in the struggle for justice and liberation for everyone, regardless of sex, class, race, nationality, or religion. Although this feminist tradition of wo/men's religious authority, agency, and friendship remains fragmented and has not always completely overcome the limitations and prejudicial frameworks of its own time and social location, its critical knowledge and continuing vibrancy

---

[39] Like other Anglo-Saxon suffragists and social reformers, Elizabeth Cady Stanton was determined but limited by her social status and class position. She not only expressed anti-immigrant sentiments by arguing that the suffrage of wo/men of her own class would increase the numbers of Anglo-Saxon voters but also appealed to ethnic and racial prejudices when she exhorted: "American women of wealth and refinement, if you do not wish the lower orders of Chinese, Africans, Germans, and Irish, with their low ideas of womanhood to make laws for you, demand that woman, too, shall be represented in the government" (quoted in Barbara Hilkert Andolsen, *Daughters of Jefferson, Daughters of Bootblacks: Racism and American Feminism* [Macon, GA: Mercer, 1986], 31).

[40] For discussion of this theoretical context, see, for example, A. Phillips, *Engendering Democracy* (University Park: University of Pennsylvania Press, 1991); Judith Butler and Joan. W. Scott, eds., *Feminists Theorize the Political* (New York: Routledge, 1992); Joan Cocks, *The Oppositional Imagination. Feminism, Critique, and Political Theory* (New York: Routledge, 1989); and Mary Lyndon Shanley and Carol Pateman, eds., *Feminist Interpretations and Political Theory* (Cambridge: Polity, 1991).

nevertheless remain crucial for contemporary radical democratic struggles in society and religion.

The Feminist The*logical Grounding of the Political Ekklēsia/ Kosmopolis Vision

The radical equality of the *ekklēsia in the kosmopolis of wo/men* is the*logically grounded in creation, in the conviction that all wo/men are created in the image of G*d, each and every human being is precious in Her eyes, and that all have received multifaceted gifts and powers of Divine Wisdom. In all our differences, wo/men represent the Divine here and now because wo/men are made in the Divine image and likeness. Everyone is made in the image of Divine Wisdom, who has gifted and called every individual differently. The Divine image is neither male nor female, white nor black, rich nor poor, but multicolored, multigendered, and more. As a richly gifted people, the *ekklēsia of wo/men* acts in the name of the world-community, the *kosmopolis*, in which religious, racial, class, and heterosexual markers no longer signify and legitimate status differences and relations of kyriarchal domination and subordination. As a pilgrim people, the *ekklēsia of wo/men* may fail repeatedly but continues to struggle, to live in fullness, and to realize its calling to be the radical democratic cosmopolitan "democracy to come."

Such an understanding of the *ekklēsia in the kosmopolis of wo/men* as a community of "friends in struggle" envisions society and religion as a reciprocal community of support, a dynamic alliance of equals. Its principle and horizon are a radical democratic vision and movement that create community in diversity, commonality in solidarity, and equality in freedom and love, a world-community that appreciates the other precisely as the other.

Feminist Studies in Religion and The*logy as a Science of Love and Hope

According to philosopher Charles Taylor, the social imaginary is not a set of "ideas" but a new vision of the moral order.[41] His basic thesis is that at the heart of Western modernity is a new understanding of the moral order of society. It tells us how we as individuals who come together to form a political identity should live together. The imaginary of *ekklēsia/kosmopolis of wo/men* as a friendship community of struggle signifies not only fullness of being, all-encompassing inclusivity, but also dynamic multiplicity and the convergence of many different voices. In Christian terms, it is foreshadowed in the image of Pentecost where people from different regions and cultures could understand the Spirit in their own languages. This image that invites Christian wo/men in the power of the Spirit to struggle together with wo/men from other religions and persuasions for the realization of the *kosmopolis of wo/men*, as G*d's alternative world of justice and well-being.

The Democratics of Justice and Love

Theoretically, the symbolic concepts of the imaginary *kosmopolis* and *ekklēsia of wo/men* seek to develop *democratics* as the horizon for feminist struggles in both religion and society at large. I borrow the term *democratics* from postcolonial feminist scholar Chela Sandoval, who has theorized it as one of the methods of the oppressed: "With the transnationalization of capitalism when elected officials are no longer leaders of singular nation-states but nexuses for multinational interests, it also becomes possible for citizen-subjects to become activists for a new decolonizing global terrain, a psychic terrain that can unite them with similarly positioned citizen-subjects within and across national borders into new, post-Western empire alliances."[42]

---

[41] Charles Taylor, "On Social Imaginary," http://web.archive.org/web/2004101 9043656/http://www.nyu.edu/classes/calhoun/Theory/Taylor-on-si.htm.
[42] Chela Sandoval, *Methodology of the Oppressed* (Minneapolis: University of Minnesota Press, 2000), 183.

She thus proposes a "methodology of the oppressed, a set of technologies for decolonizing the social [and religious] imagination" which are guided by "democratics, the practitioners' commitment to the equal distribution of power."[43]

Furthermore, Sandoval understands "love as social movement" enacted by global coalitions of citizen-activists. However, I am somewhat hesitant to claim "love" as a revolutionary force and "oppositional social action as a mode of 'love' in the postmodern world." Although I am well aware that numerous feminists have eloquently written about the power of prophetic love in struggles for justice, I cannot forget the function of selfless "romantic love" in the violence against wo/men, or the anti-Jewish Christian valorization of the "God of Love" over and against the "Old" Testament "God of Justice."[44]

In light of this oppressive Christian history and potential of love being co-opted for the interests of neoliberal globalization, I prefer feminist ethicist Margaret Farley's notion of "just love" or "loving justice."[45] The democratics of the *ekklēsia/kosmopolis of wo/men* must be equally informed by justice. As black feminist Patricia Hill Collins has argued, "A concern with justice fused with a deep spirituality appears to be highly significant to how African-American women conceptualize critical social theory. Justice constitutes an article of faith expressed through deep feelings that move people to action. For many black feminist thinkers, justice transcends Western notions of equality grounded in sameness and uniformity."[46] Here, Collins referenced Elsa Barkley Brown, who discussed African-American wo/men's quilting as pointing to the possibility "of conceptualizing an alternative notion of justice." When quilting, black wo/men weave together "scraps of fabric from all sorts of places. Nothing is wasted, and every

---

[43] Ibid.

[44] Audre Lorde, bell hooks, Toni Morrison, Cornel West, June Jordan, Gloria Anzaldúa, Maria Lugones, Merle Woo, and Alice Walker, to name just a few.

[45] Margaret A. Farley, *Just Love: A Framework for Christian Sexual Ethics* (New York: Continuum, 2006).

[46] Hill Collins, *Fighting Words*, 248.

piece of fabric has a function and a place in a given quilt. . . . Those who conceptualize community via notions of uniformity and sameness have difficulty imagining a social quilt that is simultaneously heterogeneous, driven toward excellence, and just."[47]

The Ekklēsia/Kosmopolis of Wo/men—A Radical Democratic Space

As does Collins's concept of "the social quilt," so too the democratics of the oxymoronic construct *ekklēsia/kosmopolis of wo/men* seeks to name a feminist space in neoliberal globalization where citizen-subjects of the *kosmos* fight for justice and egalitarian relations that recognize the unique difference of each and every one. This feminist space is one where the so-called secular and religious wo/men's movements can be conceptualized not as opposites or never-meeting parallels but as a radical democratic, spiritual decolonizing space and feminist public, as a "congress" of diverse wo/men's groups and feminist movements working together for change and transformation of both society and religion. Religious feminist discourses, like legal or political feminist discourses, need to be recognized as common feminist sites of political struggles not only over gender differences but also over other forms of kyriarchal domination such as racism, colonialism, or capitalism. Thus, the split between societal and religious and between biblical and postbiblical feminisms could be overcome in the interest of the diverse struggles for religious and political rights, the equalization of power, and changing relations of domination in and outside religion.

At the intersection of a multiplicity of public feminist discourses and as a site of contested sociopolitical contradictions, feminist alternatives, and unrealized possibilities, the expressions *ekklēsia* and *kosmopolis of wo/men* require a rhetorical-political rather than an ontological-essentializing conceptualization of feminist movements and studies in religion. Feminist discourses are best

---

[47] Ibid.

understood in the classical sense of deliberative rhetoric that seeks to adjudicate arguments and persuade the democratic assembly of the *kosmopolis* to make decisions for the sake of the welfare of everyone. Such a radical democratic, cosmopolitan spirituality of *ekklēsia* that feminists around the globe articulate and live every day, I submit, is able to sustain hope in our variegated struggles for a radically different democratic future. Such a rearticulation of biblical religions in terms of radical democratic equality is also necessary if religion is to become an influence and power for radical democracy. The *ekklēsia/kosmopolis of wo/men* seek to realize this vision of G*d's renewed creation by working for a radical democratic society that does not have any hungry, strangers, or outcasts but cherishes the earth and struggles in solidarity with those who are oppressed by racism, nationalism, poverty, neocolonialism, or heterosexism.

Modernity has removed the powerful analogies between kings/lords/masters/fathers and the Divine and has articulated an alternative G*d-presence. Whereas in the premodern phase G*d or some higher reality is an "ontic necessity," in the contemporary world G*d and religion are not absent from public space as secularization theory often assumes. Rather, they can be seen as inescapable sources for people to gain the power to impart order and meaning to their lives, both individually and socially. As *citizens* not only of a nation but also of the *kosmopolis*, everyone is created in G*d's image and hence represents the Divine here and now.

Religious World Making

Religious world making is difficult but possible.[48] Feminist studies in religion and the*logy have the means to imagine and to articulate the "not yet" of a domination- and violence-free, just world. The*logy as speaking about the Divine is usually understood as the science of faith. As such, it attempts to adhere to historically congealed experience and

---

[48] Compare with Darlene M. Juschka, "General Introduction," in Juschka, *Feminism in the Study of Religion*, 18, with reference to William E. Paden, *Religious Worlds: The Comparative Study of Religion* (Boston: Beacon, 1994).

thought, to scripture and tradition that seek to preserve such ideolog-ical traditions as the truth of faith and to explore its efficacious power for today. In so doing, it overlooks that traditional truth not only always already speaks the language of kyriarchy but also continues to inscribe historical structures of domination. It, therefore, becomes necessary that a critical political feminist the*logy of liberation artic-ulate the*legein as science of hope that seeks to realize change and transformation through critique and new perspectives. Feminist stud-ies in religion and the*logy as a "science of hope" seek to imagine the domination and violence free world G*d intended and to envision it repeatedly anew with the help of religious traditions and language.

Whereas *faith* often is understood as believing in something as true that excludes other religious perspectives, *hope* refers to the desire for something we lack; to the longing for justice, happiness, and well-being; and to the yearning for a different, more just world and future. That hope is something delicate and fragile, something that can van-ish and succumb to despair, is expressed in the words of Jewish-Ger-man poet Hilde Domin: "The longing for justice does not decrease, but hope does. The yearning for peace does not, but hope does."[49]

Hope requires strength, defiance, and vision; it needs, I would say, religion in order to remain alive. Religion is a slippery concept that is differently defined and understood—no generally accepted definition of religion exists. Thus, for a critical feminist the*logy, the understanding of religion as "world making" or "world creating" is important. Religion and the*logy rely on existing symbolic systems and myths for such a process of world making. In and through sym-bolic actions and imagination, religion creates again and again a world of grace different from our present world of injustice and vio-lence.

Such an understanding of religion does not conceive of tran-scendence as "hereafter" but envisions it as an alternative world of

---

[49] "Die Sehnsucht nach Gerechtigkeit nimmt nicht ab, aber die Hoffnung. Die Sen-sucht nach Frieden nicht, aber die Hoffnung" (my translation).

G*d that radically questions and challenges the systems of domination and the injustices of our present world. Language is the means to realize such a radically different imagination. However, it must not be overlooked that religious language, as all other language, has a double effect: it can either mirror our historical-kyriarchal world and religiously legitimate the status quo or it can articulate an alternative world of justice and love and proclaim it as G*d's intended world.

A Hermeneutics of Vision and Hope

The imagery of both worlds—the kyriarchal world of domination, violence, and injustice, on the one hand, and of a kyriarchy-free, divine world of well-being, justice, and love, on the other—is linguistically inscribed in holy scriptures and formative traditions. Hence, it is the task of feminist studies in religion and the*logy to develop a hermeneutic of vision and hope, which is able to differentiate between these two very different worlds and to evaluate them critically. It must repeatedly ask, What kind of world does religion proclaim? How is the Divine imagined? To what ends is the name of G*d (mis)used? and What is religious accountability for the kyriarchal exploitation and colonial injustices of our world?

Such critical querying and imagining is necessary so that religious proclamation, ritual, and ethics are able to annunciate the nonviolent, divine world of justice, well-being, and love. I argue that all religious discourses, not just Christian the*logy, have to learn how to understand themselves as a science of loving justice and hope. If feminist scholars of religion and the*logy want to proclaim a domination-free alternative world of G*d effectively and to continue such proclamation in the future, they need to engage intentionally in the process of religious and ethical "world making," of developing an ecofeminist imagination of hope in the emancipatory struggles for a more just world of love, beauty, and well-being. Latin American feminist the*logian Ivone Gebara poetically expressed this ecofeminist hope and vision for those who suffer from air pollution and a lack of pure water and green spaces:

> Beyond what is imagined by reason, there is something imagined by desire, poetry, beauty. . . . It is beautiful in its fragility and everything beautiful has something fragile in it. . . . This eschatology comingled with earth, the cycle of life, the year's seasons, the bodies of animals, plants and flowers, this human and larger than human eschatology, warms the heart a great deal.[50]

While such a vision and hope must be renewed every day and hour, the whole of creation as well as the *kosmopolis of wo/men* cry out for it

---

[50] Ivone Gebara, *Out of the Depth: Women's Experience of Evil and Salvation* (Minneapolis, MN: Fortress, 2002), 4.

CHAPTER 4

Roundtable Metalogue

This final chapter opens a new conversation among young feminists who will define future feminist theory and enact feminist transformations in different spaces and locations. Rather than defining this last chapter as an epilogue (usually a summary and conclusion) or even as a metalogue[1] (a conversation about a theoretical subject—a communication about communication as I have done in my book *Democratizing Biblical Studies*[2]), I prefer to call it a *roundtable metalogue*, which continues to situate the book's analyses in conversation with other feminist theoretical voices beyond those discussed in the footnotes. Here, students from my fall 2014 Feminist Theories and The*logies graduate seminar engage with one another and with future readers of this book. In the seminar were nine participants from different cultural and religious backgrounds who gathered around the table to explore feminist theories and the*logies: two Master of Theological Studies (MTS) and two Master of Divinity (MDiv) students from Harvard, one Master of Sacred Theology (STM) student from Boston College, one Master of Sacred Theology (STM) student from

---

[1] According to Karen Staller, "metalogues" are sites or locations where boundaries of acceptable scholarship are negotiated and standards of good scientific practices are articulated. See Karen Staller, "Metalogue as Methodology," *Qualitative Social Work* 6, no. 2 (2007): 137–57.

[2] *Democratizing Biblical Studies: Toward an Emancipatory Educational Space* (Louisville, KY: Westminster John Knox, 2009), 169–206.

Boston University, and three doctoral students, two from Harvard and one from Boston University.

While the students had differing religious and academic backgrounds and interests as well as various levels of engagement with feminist work, all critically explored feminist theories and the*logies. Some students were new to feminist work; others had a long history of engagement with it. Thus, this roundtable metalogue continues our conversations by inviting readers to participate in our discussions and dialogues on feminist theoretical and the*logical studies. The chapter also seeks to move from theory to praxis by reflecting on the communicative practices developed in the seminar. Participants in the roundtable metalogue approach the overall topic in terms of their own interests and from different thematic and methodological angles. They are not just theorizing justice and well-being but also envisioning and elaborating existing critical cosmopolitan feminist places or interconnected global intellectual spaces for feminist studies and struggles that do not exclude religion but seek to transform it.

Thus, the chapter moves from feminist theory to concrete dialogical experiences and practices. It presents a collaborative effort to reflect on the explorations of the various topoi of feminist theories and the*logies and their significance for different theoretical and the*logical areas of discussion. In short, this metalogue seeks to open up the discussion of the book for future feminist work.

Finding (My) Feminist

Heather McLetchie-Leader

As a black woman, I never wanted to be "a feminist." It is not that I wanted to be "womanist"—although I have always found Alice Walker's definition, with its emphasis on choice and *all* people, deeply appealing. Rather, I felt that as a black woman, the terms *angry*, oppositional, and aggressive were always already being read onto my body. I did not want to add to that by labeling myself *feminist*. What kinship, then, might *this* woman have with feminism?[3]

In her introduction to *Congress of Wo/men: Religion, Gender, and Kyriarchal Power*, Elisabeth Schüssler Fiorenza reflects on what brought her to feminism. For her, it was a political understanding of religious community and a commitment to changing the exclusionary teachings and structures of the religious space where she was at home that drew her to feminism's political framework and power to change. Schüssler Fiorenza does several critical things here. She affirms the multiplicity of feminism. She affirms her locatedness and the a priori commitments that shape her engagements with feminism. She affirms that her approach to the study of religion is political. She affirms the personal nature of her political involvement. She affirms her interestedness.

I, too, am interested. My location shapes my interestedness even as that interestedness shapes my location. *I know as I am known*. For me, feminism is simultaneously the most obvious choice and non-choice. I grew up *before*, in a time when feminism had yet to be turned into a caricature of itself. When *feminist* was not yet shorthand for antagonistic and man-hating—before feminist made it onto the ballot for *TIME* magazine's "word banishment" poll.[4] I do say this not in

---

[3] See Alice Walker, *In Search of Our Mothers' Gardens: Womanist Prose* (San Diego, CA: Harcourt Brace Jovanovich, 1983), xi–xii. Walker offers the following definition of "womanist": 1. From *womanish* (opp. of "girlish," i.e., frivolous, irresponsible, not serious.) . . . Usually referring to outrageous, audacious, courageous, or *willful* behavior. Wanting to know more and in greater depth than is considered "good" for one. . . . Responsible. In charge. *Serious*. 2. Also: A woman . . . [c]ommitted to survival and wholeness of entire people, male and female. Not a separatist, except periodically, for health. Traditionally universalist, as in: "Mama, why are we brown, pink, and yellow, and our cousins are white, beige, and black?" Ans.: "Well, you know the colored race is just like a flower garden, with every color flower represented." Traditionally capable, as in: "Mama, I'm walking to Canada and I'm taking you and a bunch of other slaves with me." Reply: "It wouldn't be the first time." 3. Loves music. Loves dance. Loves the moon. Loves the Spirit. Loves love and food and roundness. Loves struggle. Loves the folk. Loves herself. *Regardless*. 4. Womanist is to feminist as purple to lavender.

[4] For the past four years, *Time* has conducted a poll of which word to "ban" in the upcoming year. This year, the word *feminist* was included alongside such words as *influencer*, *bossy*, and *disrupt*. For the poll, see Katy Steinmetz, "Which Word Should Be Banned in 2015?" *Time*, November 12, 2014, http://time.com/3576870/worst-words-poll-2014.

any nostalgic way, but rather to speak to what I have seen of power and language and stereotype. No doubt, the contemporary discourse continues in its attempts to relegate feminism in all its diversity to such a narrow range of representations—not to mention, the proverbial dustbin of history. My own being is not exempt from such tactics and it is in this realization—in this witnessing to systemic strategies of silencing and erasure—that I encounter the promise of feminism for my work.

Feminist is as feminist does. One can call oneself feminist or one can be feminist. The two are neither mutually exclusive nor unrelated, but they are distinct. Read in this way, *feminist* resists attempts to pin it down. It is many things and what it looks like to be feminist means different things to different people at different times in different places and spaces. *Feminist* for me represents a sociohistorical struggle over meaning. It is semiotic, rhetorical, political. Thus, as I write, I note that I have dropped the article, substituting adjective for noun, even as I attempt to grapple with what all this might mean for me. In the absence of the article—in this *indefinition*—I no longer see a normatively defined individual. In place of identity, I see orientation, collective *noncollectivized* commitment to engaging and imagining the world in a particular way and to working toward that peculiar imaginary: to making present the subjunctive. I choose *feminist*, then, no more than I choose *black* or *woman*. The implications here are twofold. First, those who (recursively and discursively) read my *corpus* will form their own conclusions, irrespective of what I call myself. Second, the decision to declaim myself feminist or not is mostly a matter of political exigency. As I understand *feminist*, for better *and* for worse, I am that I am. I would have it no other way.

As I have worked to clarify my commitments and situatedness in relation to feminism, Schüssler Fiorenza's voice in *Congress of Wo/men: Religion, Gender, and Kyriarchal Power* has proven itself a tremendous thought partner in finding my own. As a model of feminist scholarship, the text has called me to think of feminism less in terms of its discursive loadedness and more fully in terms of its value and multiplicity as a mode of inquiry into the processes that produce and sustain difference and otherness in the world. *Feminist* more broadly pays attention to power and how power repeatedly divides the world into so many value-signified parts. In this light, the value of a kyriarchal-intersectional-feminist politics, as Schüssler Fiorenza advances, becomes clear. *Feminist* is to be concerned not just with gender but with difference; not just with identity but with the ways in which essentialized identities are mobilized to systematically include and exclude, as well as to limit self-definition for both individuals and collectives. *Feminist* is concerned with survival; it cannot help but be concerned with justice.

For Schüssler Fiorenza, this broader concern with justice has implications not only for the research programs of feminist scholars in religion but also for feminist studies more broadly construed. Schüssler Fiorenza therefore calls for greater attention to and engagement with the work of feminist theoreticians in religion. Religion, in this view, speaks not only to *religious* but also to *society*—of which religious is *a* part rather than *apart*. Thus, against an imputed secular-religious divide, her book not only interrogates political and religious structures of domination but also explores the possibilities of religious space as a political feminist space for change and transformation. Religious issues are social issues.

I am reminded throughout Schüssler Fiorenza's work that *feminist* is a construct, variously represented and marshaled to do work. To acknowledge this is not to dismiss it—though, for some, it might serve that purpose. Here, however, "constructed" helps me see the *society* embedded within. As feminist, I follow in the way (*tao*? *sunna*?) of feminist others with whom and with whose work I find affinity and kinship, who themselves follow in the way of still others. These ways are fluid, changeable, various, arcing always toward an understanding of justice. Indeed, what I have most appreciated about the text is the way it has helped me reconceptualize feminism as a temporal-historical-political phenomenon. I understand feminism with respect to the recursive-discursive formulation, fragmentation, and reformulation of sets of priorities that both generate, and are generative of, ethical-political contingency. The particularity of the vision for feminist studies in religion that Schüssler Fiorenza articulates in *Congress of Wo/men: Religion, Gender, and Kyriarchal Power* makes this clear. Though what is required in a given moment may not be "my mother's feminism," what *is* required and its articulation can be understood to build on a variegated past in ways inflected by the political necessities of the now—and of the not-yet as revealed in and by the light of the now. Thus, one understands both the moment and its requirements as articulations, persuasions: political, rhetorical, interested—and no less significant for so being.

The now-not-yet that Schüssler Fiorenza divines catches my own light in a peculiar way. She advances the need for feminist studies *in* religion ("in" as distinct from "of") that offer radical feminist critique of the kyriarchal roots of religious traditions that goes beyond the dismissal of women's religiosity as false consciousness or apology of the kyriarchal religious status quo. Her vision (prophetically) situates exigency within the global injustice of neoliberal capitalism, demanding a reconceptualizing of feminist studies in religion so that they can simultaneously challenge injustice and inspire women to struggle for survival and transformation. Thus, what she calls for is a feminist research program in religion that integrates "historical," "literary," and "the*logical"/"ethical" modalities to articulate a radical democratic religious imaginary, at the same time that it attends critically to the functioning of academic research, religious rhetoric, and other public discourses in maintaining global violence and injustice. My own work, which explores how early Christian writings mobilize marriage—and do so against the backdrop of Roman imperial legislation—attempts to orient itself in this way. My analysis of the ancient context therefore pays attention to power and kyriarchy—in particular, to the functioning of the discourse in establishing and maintaining and challenging structures of discrimination and exploitation, while raising questions about the various interests served in the representation of marriage, both at the level of the text and of the discipline. In this regard, my politics connects me to modern struggles over marriage and does so in ways that prioritize questions of survival, self-determination, and justice.

Schüssler Fiorenza then provides an excellent framework within which I can think about my work. The simple truth is that we, the scholars, are not all doing the same thing. I value Schüssler Fiorenza's work for the ways in which it flies in the face of a dangerous totalizing positivism that would assert itself as all there is.[5] And yet, the indeterminacy that her radically democratic ethos takes seriously can be difficult to sit with at times—particularly when one is called to sit among positivists; even more so when one's own inner-positivist comes calling. No doubt, this critical practice takes practice. Thankfully, it also takes place in community.

Thus, as I have wrestled with the question of whence and for whom I study *in* religion, Schüssler Fiorenza's text has been transformative. Not only has it contributed to my reflections on my research and its politics but as a pedagogy it has also been invaluable to my thinking about how I work toward the world that I dream. This includes my responsibility as a teacher and scholar in religion to create spaces that engender wholeness and well-being in testament to the multiplicity of ways that we come to knowing and knowing of "the divine" and of the historically forged link between the two. In this regard, as in others, Elisabeth Schüssler Fiorenza continues to be a tremendous teacher-mentor-advocate-guide—a feminist in whose wisdom way I am both honored and privileged to walk.

Engaging the Gospel of Femininity

Monica Rey

Schüssler Fiorenza's reflection on her own philosophical development mirrors that of many of us who have been drawn to feminism after recognizing the hierarchical and kyriarchal structuring of our own religious spaces.[6] I myself desired liberation from these kyriar-

---

[5] I use the word *positivism* here in the sense of a claim to authoritative, disinterested, "scientific" truth.

[6] "Introduction," *Congress of Wo/men: Religion, Gender, and Kyriarchal Power.*

chal structures, and this work helped me confront and begin to heal parts of myself that are still negatively affected by these spaces. In the chapter entitled "Essentializing Gender—Theologizing Gender Identity," Schüssler Fiorenza explores the ways in which the "gospel of femininity" is used within both right-wing Christian circles and also Catholic hierarchy to reduce women's roles and opportunities. This gospel of femininity envisions the good news for women as subordinate identity "modeled after the cultural ideal of the White Lady" (95).

Schüssler Fiorenza discusses the impact of the cultural ideal of the White Lady, demonstrating its far-reaching impact. Her articulation of this gospel of femininity provided the language and perspective I needed to finally address and articulate the ways in which I had been religiously socialized in my (formerly) Reformed Evangelical complementarian theological background. At the time, I did not challenge the kyriarchy of my Reformed Evangelical theological foundation, but over time, particularly after attending an evangelical seminary and serving as a pastor's wife, I could no longer ignore the ways in which these kyriarchal ideologies negatively affected women and fed into larger kyriarchal structural systems both in religious settings and in the wider American society.

One example of these kyriarchal ideologies is the doctrine of the eternal subordination of the Son (Jesus). Well-known in more conservative (fundamentalist) Reformed Evangelical circles, the eternal subordination of the Son is commonly used as an analogy for understanding complementarianism and the subordinate identity of women. Complementarianism is the belief that women and men have "complementary" roles and responsibilities in the institutions of marriage and religion. The roles prescribed for women primarily involve caretaking and submitting to the husband in all decisions. Women are also restricted from various religious leadership positions such as preaching and teaching, becoming elders, or being recognized as deacons. All of this further becomes moralized as "duty," and married women are asked to "submit" to their husbands because that is their complementary role in much the same way Jesus himself modeled his own submissive position to the Father. The doctrine of the eternal subordination of the Son, therefore, argues that Jesus *eternally* submits his will to the Father in their relationship to each other in the Godhead.

Women, then, are indoctrinated to follow this example of Jesus by submitting to their husbands. As a result, this kyriarchal ideology serves to promote essentialized feminine identity as a subordinate identity, thereby facilitating women's domination. Finally, it is even more problematic given that many women are financially unable to fulfill their "duty" of performing the gospel of femininity but are nevertheless punished by sexist workplace politics.[7] As a Latina, this principle is even more problematic in that status and class and race are, as Schüssler Fiorenza points out, inflected and overlooked when gender is essentialized.

I was first introduced to this concept of the gospel of femininity by my campus minister who was stepping down to pursue motherhood full time. At the time, her decision was lauded and admired as fulfilling her feminine (religious) duty. Growing up lower middle class with my mother, who worked the late-night shift at McDonald's or hours at Dunkin' Donuts to make ends meet for my brother and me, made this religiously noble pursuit of full-time motherhood foreign to me. In this way, my Peruvian mother stood outside the gender essentialism promoted by this conservative religious ideology, which envisioned my mother as a failure.

As Schüssler Fiorenza demonstrates in this book, the gospel of femininity "attempts to defend the privileges of white middle- and upper-class women who, until the globalization of markets, had the privilege of not having to work outside the home" (96) while marking those who cannot afford or are structurally barred from doing so as religiously and socially inferior. Thus, Schüssler Fiorenza has

---

[7] Bryce Covert, "Melissa Harris-Perry on the Politics and Pitfalls of Motherhood in America," last modified March 10, 2014, http://thinkprogress.org/econ-omy/2014/03/10/3382941/mhp-motherhood/.

helped me see the ways in which the kyriarchal principle of the "essentialized feminine identity as subordinated identity" or the "gospel of femininity" exceeds the religious settings in which it is mobilized and actually has much further-reaching effect on women's lives worldwide (Chapter 2).

Engaging the Oikonomia ("the Economy") in the Ekklēsia of Wo/men

Melody Stanford

In seminar discussions that wrestled with a vision of radical feminist democracy, the questions that arose were often What can we actually *do?* and Where do we go from here? Hence, I would like to turn our attention to the material world of economic exchange and spend more time considering how deeply economy influences the issues this book articulates. Indeed, resource manipulation has historically functioned, and continues to function, as *the* primary mode of transportation for kyriarchy.

In an age where corporations are considered people, the *kosmopolis* is increasingly shaped by purchasing power: the ability to sanction and unsanction. Elite private sector rule, in the global phenomenon of transnational corporatocracy, functions as deeply antidemocratic. In this reality, local markets are seductively and violently shunted to make space for neocolonial, neoliberal, econolegal technologies that champion the wants of the few over the needs of the many. Political systems that ought to ensure the flourishing of human life are beholden, coerced, or indebted into complicity with the demands of the neoliberal marketplace. Globalist profit mongering is dependent on maintaining the status quo for certain hierarchies, which means age-old cultural constructions of race, gender, and class are not, by all accounts, diminishing, but instead growing stronger. Hiding and shape-shifting within social orders, innovations of cultural, legal, and environmental rape are prized. Consuming human life through economic modes has arguably become a religion—complete with canon, doctrine, saints, and rituals—a religion that hinges on a soteriology of "too big to fail" perpetual growth.

Nowhere is this better depicted than in cases of environmental "privatization." A prescient example in recent years is the case of water rights in Bolivia. Bolivian activists, under the leadership of Evo Morales, won a decade-long battle to establish a legal foundation for water as a basic human right. With scarce resources to counter the seemingly bottomless purse strings of transnational corporations, native peoples successfully challenged corporate insistence that "water is a product among other consumables that may be monetized."[8]

Is it not a form of genocide to hinder a community's ability to survive by annihilating people's *access* to the water necessary to live? Not only is water the basis for organic life but also in Christian traditions, as in many other religions, fresh water is a symbol for the Divine as well as for peace, healing, and inclusion. Yet, rarely do religious communities actively decry malicious practices of neoliberal globalist corporations—even when those who suffer most during these atrocities are the "least of these": the millions of wo/men and children who have the *least* mobility, *least* access to governmental protection, and *least* access to resources. This question of environmental and economic genocide is applicable for every instance when a person is denied basic necessities for life.

---

[8] Emily Achtenberg, "From Water Wars to Water Scarcity: Bolivia's Cautionary Tale," June 5, 2013, North American Congress on Latin America (NACLA), https://nacla.org/blog/2013/6/5/water-wars-water-scarcity-bolivia's-cautionary-tale. Unfortunately, Bolivia is still locked in an intense struggle to develop infrastructure that can address internal scarcities and entanglements with foreign aid. This is not a simple David and Goliath victory; outcomes in the quest to conquer corporatocracy are often muddled, as the immensity of modern globalism compels all systems into its likeness. In her book *Just Water: Theology, Ethics, and the Global Water Crisis* (Maryknoll, NY: Orbis, 2014), Christiana Z. Peppard, expresses astonishment that this battle had to be fought at all, especially to the extent of having to involve the United Nations. This kind of public-private collusion is beyond a neglectful practice of polluting rivers, for example, though such issues are also grave. Environmental "privatization," in particular, marks a pattern that is far more insidious. It represents a set of ideologies that allow those who have resources to justify the pursuit of excess over and against the existences of those who must strive for basic survival.

While religious communities often concern themselves with providing immediate forms of aid, rarely do these same communities deeply investigate or take real action against larger systemic practices like environmental violence; monopolistic or oligarchical collusion in industries like medicine, military contracting, higher education, and oil; patent trolling; or debt extortion. Certainly, many individuals and organizations find motivation in their faiths to resist such injustices, but the prevailing ideologies of neoliberalism inculcate notions that such economic abuses are, in fact, "secular" or "para-religious" problems.

In light of this, what does it mean for wo/men to build an *ekklēsia* that moves radical democracy forward? It means inquiring into new visions of economy and sustainability. The word *economy* originated from the Greek *oikonomia*, or "the management of the household," a notion that includes not only the legal and the material world of exchange but also the spirit—the assumptions, values, and rhetoric of how the *oikos* functions, and how we as a human family navigate the household of the world. Economics, as a study of justice, is as fundamental to democratic society as water or air is fundamental to survival and the flourishing of life. Ultimately, moral failure will be the end of neoliberal capitalism. Processes of expansive consumption are limited in a finite world, and resistance to long-term sustainability will be its own undoing.[9] In the meantime, the costs incurred for the rest of us may be utterly insurmountable.

This is what makes the work of the *ekklēsia of wo/men* so robust. Consider the widely interdisciplinary nature of the *ekklēsia* project. The participation of each citizen is necessary; only a collective of individual perspectives, experiences, knowledges, and voices, in all spheres of life, can truly break dualistic and essentializing rituals, which seek to dismember what is, in truth, a radically interconnected *kosmopolis*. When we refuse to view existence in terms of disjunctive

---

[9] Kent A. Klitgaard and Lisi Krall, "Ecological Economics, Degrowth, and Institutional Change," *Ecological Economics* 84, no 1 (2012): 247–53.

and hierarchical divisions, when we refuse to see ourselves and all of our dealings as being in any way separate from the earth, we lean into utterly creative and life-giving ways of being and interacting. As we practice right relationship with the *kosmos*, we investigate the values that dance us forward. We peer into connections between bodies of knowledge that have historically been held apart, such as theology and economy. We challenge the strangleholds of abusive institutions by unraveling artificial conditions of sanctioned spaces and actions.

Feminists have historically done this kind of work in two ways. First, feminists and those who have been inspired by feminist legacy have actively challenged the rhetorical as inseparable from language.[10] From Virginia Woolf to Luce Irigaray to Mary Daly to Elisabeth Schüssler Fiorenza, feminist theory and the*logy have demonstrated that language *creates* realities. Effectively challenging kyriarchy means challenging all genres of information and knowledge—including the "objective"/scientific, the narrative, the legal and political, the mythic—any ideology that hegemony seeks to weaponize. Kyriarchal power shelters itself in complexity, anonymity, and in terms of the "official." To engage the rhetorical is to toy with, tease out, innovate, and ultimately assert collective spatial sharing of communication and meaning.

Second, feminists have organized and connected. In the aftermath of so-called wo/men's liberation in the 1970s, consciousness-raising groups sprang up in unsanctioned and sanctioned spaces around the globe.[11] Many scholars who write on consciousness-raising groups characterize three broad functions that sprang from rhetorical theory: 1) recovering of lost or silenced "texts" (including texts of selves and experiences); 2) naming and analyzing oppressions (conscientization); and 3) exploring possibilities of political action. There is some variance in approach to consciousness-raising. Indeed, goals

---

[10] Elisabeth Schüssler Fiorenza, *Democratizing Biblical Studies: Toward an Emancipatory Educational Space* (Louisville, KY: Westminster John Knox, 2009), 73–76.

[11] Ibid., 15.

and processes differ among generations and communities. Some scholars engage consciousness-raising specifically in development of "third wave" feminism,[12] while others focus on consciousness-*building* through the development of coalitions, resisting notions of safety in favor of crossing hard boundaries of difference.[13]

Still another perspective, informed by progressive workers in the "majority world," uses the term *consciousness-awakening*. In a recent article exploring the work of "activist-healer" health workers in Latin America, Chicana scholar Irene Lara offers the benefits of a model that deconstructs mind-body dualism and decenters Western intellectualism and individualism. This is a model in which organizers are not experts but rather "healers in need of healing" who offer resources and support and facilitate co-learning.[14]

Instead of seeing consciousness as something imposed from an outside source (as subject formation might be viewed as incomplete), the "awakening" model offers that there is no foundational lack, and holds that wo/men agency is often, and to some degree, in a state of dormancy. As such, individuals and groups co-learn—in developing language and the ability to critically engage the rhetorical and the ideological, they are able to move forward in political action from the basis of community, solidarity, and friendship. This consciousness-awakening and acting work is an embodiment of the spirit of *ekklēsia*. Though the frequency of these groups has diminished in recent decades, emerging global technologies provide opportunities for new iterations of these practices.

Challenging the rhetorical and acting in community are two practical, on-the-ground charges for the road ahead. In addition to the legacy of feminist activism, a third task is emerging. In order to *be* the

---

[12] Sowards and Renegar, "Rhetorical Functions of Consciousness Raising," 535–52.
[13] Karlyn Kohrs Campbell, "Consciousness-Raising: Linking Theory, Criticism, and Practice," *Rhetoric Society Quarterly* 32, no. 1 (2002): 45–64; see also Cricket Keating, "Building Coalitional Consciousness," *NWSA Journal* 17, no. 2 (2005): 86–103; and Sowards and Renegar, "Rhetorical Functions of Consciousness Raising."
[14] Irene Lara, "Latina Health Activist-Healers Bridging Body and Spirit," *Women and Therapy* 31, no. 1 (2008): 21–40.

religiopolitical *ekklēsia*, we must educate ourselves to speak meaning-fully into the *oikonomia*—the ways in which we act out our values through relating to one another. This should be particularly true for US and European thinkers who are situated closest to the controls of the commanding heights of empire.

We need to develop viable alternatives to genocidal and gynoci-dal capitalism, and new economic systems of equality, hospitality, and sharing. We need to consolidate a new globalist ethics that will encourage holistic, sustainable provision of basic needs for all. We need to turn attention to strengthening global structures that will enforce the enactment of such ethics. We need to restore our crea-turely connection with the earth in order that we might heal it—and ourselves—in the process. Finally, we need to build bridges, particu-larly, for those who recognize the deeply the*logical implications of this kind of work, that our discourse remains coherent and accessible to those who work from different perspectives.

Throughout the task of dismantling kyriarchy and designing a better reality, we work to radically resist and reconfigure kyriarchal structures that regard life as consumable. Such systems are our tragic inheritance: the mythos of the self *pitted against* the collective, the hierarchical dualisms that fuel "legitimacies," and the many enabling religious institutions that neglect their prophetic voices. Being the *ekklēsia* begins with the examination of our modes of relationship and exchange; such reveal our foundational values. The work ahead will require a great deal of creativity.

A Reframing of Feminist Theology: Moving beyond Gender Binaries

Ashley Unruh

For as long as I can remember, I have considered myself to be a *feminist* in the most basic sense of the term (believing in the equality of wo/men) and through the Feminist Theories and The*logies semi-nar, I was able to explore the ways in which feminist the*logy pro-vides a platform of liberation and empowerment. This perspective allowed me to explore the adage that religion oppresses wo/men, and this seminar addressed this question directly and unapologetically. Through the process of reviewing *Congress of Wo/men: Religion, Gender, and Kyriarchal Power*, I was challenged to reframe my ideas about feminist theory and the*logy in ways that I never imagined, such as problematizing the essentialization of gender. Instead of problematizing gender theory in binary terms, this book proposes that we examine gender in relationship to race, class, and other positions of power. By framing gender within the larger context of power domination, *Congress of Wo/men* provided me with the language to articulate feminist the*logy as a transformative methodology.

At the beginning of the semester, we were asked to establish goals in order to articulate what we brought into the classroom and where we hoped to end up. Now, reflecting on the seminar and the goals that I set out to accomplish, I better understand why we were asked to articulate our goals in this way. As Elisabeth Schüssler Fiorenza acknowledges in this book, "one always already has a pre-understanding of the subject matter that one seeks to understand" (12) and I came into this class with a preset understanding of feminist theory and the*logy as framing domination solely in terms of gender hegemony.

After spending a great deal of time studying feminist theory through a legal framework, I had cautiously decided to engage feminist theory through a religious/the*logical lens. This was not an area of feminist theory with which I was completely comfortable, but after studying how the legal system criminalized sex workers based on laws that express religious ideals of morality, I felt convinced that I needed to study feminist theory through a the*logical framework as a way to equip myself to completely frame the paradigm of the institution of prostitution.

In *Congress of Wo/men: Religion, Gender, and Kyriarchal Power*, Schüssler Fiorenza argues that systems of power are defined by a number of intersecting structures of domination. If systems of power represent a number of factors such as race, class, and education, then dualistic frameworks of gender identity become problematic. Instead of viewing oppression in terms of men over women, Schüssler Fiorenza asks us to view power and oppression through multiple lenses, in which the identities of wo/men are experienced through different structural and subject positions. By challenging the sufficiency of gender as an analytical category in this regard, Schüssler Fiorenza offers a new perspective through which scholars can critically engage oppression by means of a the*logical framework.

The kyriarchal framework that is introduced not only questions the oppression of religious ideologies but also seeks to understand these ideologies in concert with political principles that oppress wo/men. By doing this, Schüssler Fiorenza asks feminist scholars to engage religious studies as a serious tool to counter neoliberal assertions that claim feminism "wages against religion" (9). This method of feminist studies is "future-oriented," as it seeks "to name the reality of wo/men's oppression, to encourage actions of empowerment and liberation, and again and again to articulate anew such a vision of well-being" (7). This transformative vision, which became a constant focus in our classroom debates, resonated with me throughout the seminar and ultimately became the focus of my final paper.

At the end of the semester, as I read the goals I had established at the beginning, one in particular resonated with me: I want to raise my own consciousness of the privileges and struggles not only of my life but also of the lives of my classmates, in order to understand how biblical interpretations have shaped my understanding of race, class, gender, and sexual orientation. From the outset, I had hoped to engage with feminist the*logy in a transformative way; however, I lacked the language that would allow me to engage the*logy in ways that could transform issues of social justice and human rights. This book, however, presented the language needed to articulate the importance of bringing a the*logical framework to feminist studies.

In Chapter 1, the importance of religious studies comes to the fore as Schüssler Fiorenza introduces the dichotomy between secular and religious ideologies in the United States. Oftentimes, these two methods ignite dualistic debates that confine women to essentialized roles. Within the framework of this book, Schüssler Fiorenza focuses on the current state of abortion in the United States. One of the most startling observations is that by criminalizing abortion, the law also criminalizes everyone involved—to Schüssler Fiorenza this is clearly a religiously charged issue that is inadequately handled by the current rhetoric of feminist theory. By negating the*logy, Schüssler Fiorenza fears that feminist theory is ill-equipped to handle the levels of domination at play in political rhetoric. This aspect of the book resonated with me as I constructed my own paper, as it illustrates the important role feminist the*logy plays in the transformative vision of the future, in which wo/men are granted full citizen rights.

A number of student papers incorporated Schüssler Fiorenza's transformative vision as a theoretical space within which to engage their own concrete calls for change. My paper focused on a kyriarchal analysis of the institution of prostitution, in order to understand the implications of intersectionality in securing full citizenship for sex workers. I used feminist the*logy as a way to articulate the importance of intersectionality in order to demonstrate the shortcomings of current feminist debates. As of now, sex workers are demonized and marginalized from all angles of domination and therefore limited in accessing full participation in a democratic society. Much like the *ekklēsia* in Schüssler Fiorenza's book, my own transformative vision seeks to incorporate feminist the*logy as a foundation that allows feminist theory to formulate solutions beyond dualistic patriarchal notions of domination and instead to engage prostitution through the lens of kyriarchy.

I contend that in order to challenge prostitution as an institution, a kyriarchal lens simultaneously represents a number of structures of domination and allows advocates and scholars to better frame a wo/man's choice to enter and remain in prostitution, rather than "either/or" approaches, such as eliminate prostitution or criminalize prostitution. Neither of these frameworks fully represents the choices and consequences that accompany the entirety of the institution of prostitution that limits a wo/man's agency. Therefore, I base my own transformative vision within the*logy, because the current political landscape demonizes sex workers as the polar opposite of the *White Lady*, a term Schüssler Fiorenza introduced. If political regimes use the White Lady as the moral foundation for criminalizing the behavior of sex workers, then feminist the*logians must alter that framework in order to provide political availability to all wo/men, regardless of perceived moral character.

In this way, Schüssler Fiorenza's theories on feminist the*logy unapologetically analyzed religion within religion (5). Many of my colleagues' papers examined religion within religion by examining scripture through a critical lens. Melody Stanford's paper, for instance, clearly demonstrated how feminist the*logy could be taught and utilized in a number of "real life" circumstances, and this articulation of feminist the*logy as inherently accessible allowed me to start envisioning different ways to use feminist the*logy. This book provided the framework and foundation for the arguments found in my paper and forced me to take seriously feminist positions that were very different from my own.

Because of this dynamic articulation of feminist the*logy, I began to question why I believed certain things and where those beliefs stemmed from. Questioning one's beliefs is central to unearthing transformative visions of equality. As a concluding thought, I believe the transformative nature of this book distinguishes it as a distinct perspective in the field of feminist studies. This book asks feminist scholars to engage religious studies in a serious way, in order to fully understand the religious implicitness of political decisions that are currently marginalizing wo/men. However, this transformative vision cannot be realized until power systems are viewed within the framework of intersecting power structures. Without this comprehensive understanding, feminist studies cannot adequately respond to injustices that kyriarchal interpretations of religion fuel.

Christian Symbols and Kyriarchal Ideology

Elyse Raby

The Feminist Theories and The*logies seminar was a dynamic site of shared learning and self-critique. As a student of Catholic systematic the*logy at the Boston College School of Theology and Ministry, a Catholic institution, I was humbled and delightfully challenged by my colleagues' range of scholarly interests; religious and denominational traditions; racial, cultural, and national identities; and active social and political commitments. In this rich environment, our seminar was a small but concrete instantiation of the collaboration among feminist theorists, the*logians, scripture scholars, scholars of religion, and community organizers that this present book invites.

Though much of Schüssler Fiorenza's scholarship uses the analytic lens of kyriarchy, it was not until I read the manuscript of *Congress of Wo/men: Religion, Gender, and Kyriarchal Power* that my prior assumptions about the necessity and utility of a sex/gender analytic in feminist theory and theology were roundly dismantled. Schüssler Fiorenza argues in Chapter 1 that the modern two-sex system functions to legitimate kyriarchal oppression. She states that "by presenting the dualistic sex/gender system of male and female or masculine and feminine as universal and essential, this frame of meaning obscures the reality that the very notion of two genders/sexes is a sociopolitical construct for maintaining domination and not a biological given or ideological essence" (43).

This essentialist perspective fails to consider fully that "gender is always already differently inflected by race, class, age, sexuality, imperialism, and other power structures" (43). If feminist theory and studies in religion remain trapped in a sex/gender framework of analysis, it cannot adequately theorize and address the devastation and oppression that kyriarchal neoliberal globalization inflicts upon wo/men.

As Schüssler Fiorenza has demonstrated throughout this book, movements such as "New Feminism," "True Womanhood," and

ENDOW leverage biblical texts, religious traditions, and the modern two-sex framework in order to justify kyriarchal systems of domination, both within church communities and in the so-called secular or political realms, and to inculcate Christian identity. Within my own field of Catholic the*logy, the oppressive potential of the*logical symbols and their reliance upon the modern sex/gender system is especially visible within Christology (the*logical reflection on Jesus/Christ[15]), a topic that I took up in my research paper for Schüssler Fiorenza's seminar.

Traditional (or "malestream") Christian the*logy regards Jesus's maleness as an ontological, the*logical, and historical necessity. As such, it has been used to subordinate wo/men, theoretically jeopardize their salvation,[16] and bar them from ordination in the Roman Catholic Church because the female sex does not bear a "natural resemblance" to Christ, "who was and remains a man."[17] Though traditional Christology is riddled with kyriarchal language (for example, Jesus/Christ as "Lord" and "King"), the modern two-sex system functions distinctively in Catholic Christology insofar as *all* men regardless of race, class, nationality, and so on—and *only* men, never women—are capable of "imaging Christ" sacramentally, though this

---

[15] I borrow Kwok Pui-lan's hybrid concept "Jesus/Christ," which indicates the "space between Jesus and Christ" that is "unsettling and fluid, resisting easy categorization and closure," when I am not making a hard distinction between the "historical Jesus" and the "resurrected Christ." See Kwok Pui-lan, *Postcolonial Imagination and Feminist Theology* (Louisville, KY: Westminster John Knox, 2005), 171.

[16] Elizabeth Johnson, "Redeeming the Name of Christ," in *Freeing Theology: The Essentials of Theology in Feminist Perspective*, ed. Catherine Mowry LaCugna (San Francisco, CA: HarperSanFrancisco, 1993), 115–27, at 119.

[17] The Holy See, "Declaration on the Question of Admission of Women to the Ministerial Priesthood *Inter Insigniores*," October 15, 1976, par. 5, http:// www.vatican.va/ roman_curia/congregations/cfaith/documents/rc_con_cfaith_doc_19761015_inter-insigniores_en.html. Susannah Cornwall notes that the same line of argument is also operative in her Anglican tradition in "Sex Otherwise: Intersex, Christology, and the Maleness of Jesus," *Journal of Feminist Studies in Religion* 30, no. 2 (2014): 23–39. Interestingly, this functions in the opposite way in some Evangelical Protestant churches, where women are called to imitate Jesus/Christ, who is eternally subordinate to the Father. I am grateful to my Feminist Theories and The*logies seminar colleague Monica Rey for bringing this to my attention.

Christ is often described in the image of the elite, white, European, powerful male.

In order to counter this historically kyriarchal tradition, contemporary feminist, postcolonial, and queer the*logians are utilizing theories of sex, gender, and intersectionality to bring female, intersex, trans, and queer embodiment to bear on Christology. In doing so, they destabilize maleness as constitutive of Jesus/Christ and offer wo/men a means by which they can identify themselves with God and Christ, inclusive of, not in spite of, their sex and gender identity. From the historical Jesus as possibly intersex,[18] to a bi/transvestite Christ-symbol,[19] to Jesus as the incarnation of Sophia-Wisdom,[20] feminist the*logies are striving toward a wide and liberating range of interpretive and symbolic possibilities within Christology. These new Christological symbols "provide alternative theoretical spaces from which to critically analyze our structural position and articulate, in tandem with such critical analyses and constructive alternative visions, the range of possible subject positions" (75).

Still, these Christologies are largely beholden to a sex/gender analysis, even as they attempt with some success to challenge the rigid and essentialist dichotomies within the modern two-sex system.[21] Feminist critiques of Jesus/Christ as "Lord" and "King," preeminent symbols of the elite, propertied, heterosexual European male, were barely uncovered in my survey of recent Christian feminist the*logy. Even Kwok Pui-Lan, in her book *Postcolonial Imagination and Feminist Theology*, presents five symbols of a postcolonial Christ (the Black Christ, Christ as Corn Mother, Christ as Feminine Shakti, Christ as

---

[18] Cornwall, "Sex Otherwise." See also Virginia Ramey Mollenkott, *Omnigender: A Trans-religious Approach* (Cleveland, OH: Pilgrim, 2001).
[19] Robert Goss, *Queering Christ: Beyond "Jesus Acted Up"* (Cleveland, OH: Pilgrim, 2002).
[20] Elizabeth Johnson, *She Who Is: The Mystery of God in Feminist Theological Discourse* (New York: Crossroad, 1992).
[21] Marcella Althaus-Reid's scholarship stands out as an exception.

Theological Transvestite,[22] and Jesus as Bi/Christ) that focus primarily on Jesus's sex/gender and only address imperialist Christological titles in a brief and introductory way.[23] In this regard, both traditional Christologies and the feminist correctives mentioned here illustrate Schüssler Fiorenza's point that the modern sex/gender system obfuscates the multiplicative embodied and social components of identity and status. Clearly, a fully intersectional analysis of the Christological tradition is still needed.

Feminist the*logians have long noted that images, symbols, and rhetorics of the Divine shape religious communities and their structures of power, domination, and exclusion; it is not surprising then that the symbol of Jesus/Christ functions as such in the Christian tradition. But beyond images of the Divine, within Christian and especially Catholic tradition images of Mary, Mother of God, must also be the site of critical and intersectional feminist analysis. Schüssler Fiorenza notes the remarkable impact that "dualistic feminine identity movements" such as "New Feminism" and "True Womanhood" have had in this country (Chapter 1). Though Schüssler Fiorenza does not explicitly mention this, I suspect that the Mariologies espoused by these movements represent the Mother of God as a spitting image of the White Lady of kyriarchal ideology and cultural bourgeois femininity. This is certainly the case in the writings of Pope John Paul II, such as *Mulieris Dignitatem* (1988) and the "Letter to Women" (1995). In fact, ENDOW explicitly takes its inspiration from these texts.[24] In these theological writings, Mary's motherhood *"determines the essential horizon of reflection on the dignity and the vocation of women,"*[25] which is summed up in biological and/or spiritual motherhood—a motherhood that is lauded as

---

[22] Susannah Heschel's image of Jesus/Christ as "theological transvestite" "unsettles and queers the boundaries between Judaism and Christianity"—her focus is not on sex/gender/sexuality binaries (cited in Kwok, *Postcolonial Imagination*, 179–80).

[23] Ibid., 168.

[24] See "About Us," ENDOW, http://endowgroups.org/about-us/.

[25] "Apostolic Letter on the Dignity and Vocation of Women *Mulieris Dignitatem*," August 15, 1988, at The Holy See, Online: http://w2.vatican.va/content/john-paul-ii/en/apost_letters/1988/documents/hf_jp-ii_apl_19880815_mulieris-dignitatem.html.

a complete and total "gift of self" and the full realization of "woman's" psychophysical and spiritual constitution.[26] Mary's own motherhood is characterized by her "handmaid" status (Luke 1:38), obedience to God, and complete loving self-sacrifice.[27] In the Roman Catholic tradition, Mary is not only the model of ideal womanhood and "the highest expression of the 'feminine genius'" but also invoked as a symbol of the Church, both in its "spiritual motherhood" as it portends Christ in and to the world and in the obedience of the whole community of faith to the Lord.[28]

Schüssler Fiorenza highlights in Chapter 2 the relationship between this idealized femininity, the wo/men's movement, and the Catholic Church's religious and political action against the accessibility of birth control and the devastating effects this ideology continues to have on the lives of wo/men, especially poor wo/men. As mentioned elsewhere in this chapter, my seminar colleague Ashley Unruh has explored the particular impact that this moral ideology has on the lives of sex workers. It is easy to see even in the cursory remarks cited above that traditional Roman Catholic Mariology sanctifies and mobilizes neoliberal and kyriarchal power and inculcates the "ethos of submission" that Schüssler Fiorenza has brought to light in this book. Clearly, then, the concrete realization of the *ekklēsia of wo/men* will require tireless resignification not just of the Divine, or of the symbolic body of Christ, but also of Mary insofar as she functions as the ideal type for womanhood and a symbol of the Christian church.

Schüssler Fiorenza concludes her text by acknowledging the power that the imaginary of the *ekklēsia of wo/men* has in providing new interpretive frameworks for wo/men's lives and *ekklēsial* communities. If she

---

[26] Ibid., §18

[27] "Letter of Pope John Paul II to Women," June 29, 1995, at The Holy See. Online: https://w2.vatican.va/content/john-paul-ii/en/letters/1995/documents/hf_jp-ii_let_29061995_women.html.

[28] In addition to the texts already mentioned, see also *Evangelium Vitae*, Online: http://w2.vatican.va/content/john-paul-ii/en/encyclicals/documents/hf_jp-ii_enc_25031995_evangelium-vitae.html §§102–105, and the Second Vatican Council's Dogmatic Constitution on the Church *Lumen Gentium*, Chap. 8, The Holy See http://www.vatican.va/archive/hist_councils/ii_vatican_council/documents/vat-ii_const_19641121_lumen-gentium_en.html.

is right in her analysis of the interplay between religion, scriptures, and neoliberal globalization, and I believe she is, feminist theorists would be remiss to ignore the work done by feminist the*logians in de- and reconstructing symbols of the Divine, Christ, and Mary.[29] It is at the level of the symbol that feminist the*logies, and especially feminist Christologies, can uniquely contribute to the creative envisioning of a radically democratic *ekklēsia of wo/men* together with critical feminist theory and transnational feminist movements. Schüssler Fiorenza's present work provides the rationale, exigency, and theoretical tools for this important collaboration.

Divine Dispersions: Toward a Feminist Imaginary of the Incarnational God

T. Rhyker Benavidez

In our graduate seminar, feminist scholars of religion from different social locations gathered together to form a radically diverse community, each person uniquely committed to envisioning and reenvisioning their particular feminist imaginary. While I greatly appreciated the various viewpoints and perspectives of my fellow classmates, we often reached impasses in our otherwise fruitful discussions. In these cases, I experienced firsthand the "feminist contradiction," the persistent reality that wo/men disagree about what is best for wo/men. During these moments, I initially grew disheartened: If even a small group of wo/men dedicated to eradicating kyriarchy cannot agree, is the project of a critical feminist the*logy of liberation doomed from the outset?

---

[29] Elizabeth Johnson has begun this work in *Truly Our Sister: A Theology of Mary in the Communion of Saints* (New York: Continuum, 2003). With regard to the church as "the body of Christ," Karen Alliaume and Laura Taylor utilize Judith Butler's theory of gender performativity to suggest that Christian discipleship and ecclesiology are better conceived as a *performance* of Christ, rather than an *imitation* of Christ, which risks excluding wo/men given the traditional insistence on Christ's eternal maleness. See Laura Taylor, "Redeeming Christ: Imitation or (Re)Citation?" in Abraham and Procario-Foley, *Frontiers in Catholic Feminist Theology*, 119–40, and her use of Alliaume therein.

On the contrary, throughout the semester, I learned that the bringing together of diverse and even contradictory viewpoints is precisely what is necessary to destabilize the kyriarchal regime. As Schüssler Fiorenza states, "[Feminist emancipatory theories] must create spaces and opportunities for very different wo/men to move across religious and social borders in order to encounter one another, to join in solidarity with one another, and to harness their power of change" (7, emphasis added). Indeed, the the*logy of liberation articulated in this publication requires that we all demand political freedom, regardless of our identity and subjectivity. This political definition of feminism resonates deeply with my own personal desires as a queer Latino Christian man struggling to live fully and unapologetically.

Surely, the dynamic assemblage of identity categories to which I ascribe, as well as those which others inscribe upon me, will always already inform my encounters with and analysis of a critical-political feminist the*logy of liberation. As Schüssler Fiorenza writes, "there is no value-neutral scholarship. Scholarship is always already situated— religiously, socially, culturally, and politically" (12). So then, Schüssler Fiorenza reminds us all of the importance in realizing the multitude of ways in which we are situated, not only as individuals, but also within larger institutional contexts. For myself, being the only male in the seminar provided me a unique perspective through which to engage with an intersectional-kyriarchal lens of analysis. Though as a queer Latino I have experienced my fair share of oppression due to kyriarchal systems, my male privilege blinded me to the pervasive ways that kyriarchal structures subjugate wo/men. Because of this, I often fell silent during the seminar, listening intently to my female colleagues as they discussed their particular experiences with and scholarship concerning kyriarchy. Thankfully, I am now better able to understand a smidgeon of what my female classmates go through on a daily basis, navigating through a world that actively excludes them from its institutions.

Entering into the seminar, Schüssler Fiorenza had us write down and share our goals for the semester. Surely, if it is true that we are enlivened by the power of [our] vision, then it is essential for us to endeavor to sketch what our "collectivized" (Heather MeLetchie Leader, "Finding My Feminist," 124 in this volume) vision is. Looking back, I realize my deeply personal aspirations and hopes that undergirded my vision. For example, one of my goals was to integrate my diverse set of identities into a coherent whole, in spite of the social pressures and tensions that cause me to believe that I am a living paradox of mutually exclusive constituents. Growing up in a fundamentalist evangelical Protestant home, I believed that I would spend eternity tormented in hell due to my sexual orientation. Thus, I seek a critical feminist the*logy of liberation to help me in my quest to reconcile these identities. Another goal I had was my hope that the seminar would allow me to experience and/or understand how the divine interacts with each one of us, especially those who are marginalized and oppressed. As someone who was told that my desires were irreconcilable with the presence of G*d, I find the concept of reimagining the divine as being co-implicated and dispersed within all of humanity to have a uniquely liberating potential.

In this vein, I believe that any critical-political feminist theory that aspires toward the liberation of all wo/men must be grounded in, or at least in dialogue with, an equally critical-political feminist the*logy. Certainly, I have found that my the*logical leanings exist a priori to my political and theoretical leanings. For those of us who regard the work of a critical-political feminism to be a crucial the*logical task, it is important to articulate an alternative imaginary concerning the divine. In this work, Schüssler Fiorenza describes her own notion of the *ekklēsia of wo/men* as "a key radical democratic, theoretical, and practical political site of such a cosmopolitan feminism" (108). While this term powerfully reorganizes human communities flourishing apart from kyriarchal systems of dominance, I believe it neglects to reenvision a notion of the divine in that same regard.

In fact, I wrote my final project for the seminar with this goal of radically opening up the divine in mind. While researching for this paper, I hoped to become better acquainted with a more diverse and representative set of voices within feminist the*logy. Thankfully, I was able to investigate sexism, homophobia, transphobia, and ableism more fully in my final paper, which analyzed non-normative embodiment with a critical queer and feminist lens. Specifically, I investigated female, queer, trans, intersex, and disabled corporeality. So doing, I was able to explore the limits and contours of discourse concerning the body, as well as to provide a the*logical imaginary on embodiment and the divine. The communal aspect of the seminar was very helpful in this regard, as my final paper was deeply enhanced by the insights I learned from Elyse Raby's paper on Christology.

Speaking from a Christian perspective, I argue in my paper that any critical-political feminist the*logy must include incarnation as a "basic theological posture."[30] As Lisa Isherwood, professor of the*logy at the University of Winchester, writes in her book *Beyond Monotheism*, the incarnation is "a concept that declares the full flourishing/ redemption of all."[31] How, then, can the concept of incarnation be extended beyond the corporeality of Jesus? To answer this question, I echo Isherwood's belief that the human and divine dwell in the same flesh and that this flesh is our own flesh.[32] In this way, we can begin to understand ourselves and our bodies as entirely divine and to understand G*d as located within ourselves and our bodies. One of the most profound applications of this notion of radical incarnation is that it forces us to realize that redemption does not occur through cosmic intervention but through passionate engagement with the world and those in it. Instead of an otherworldly eschatology, radical incarnation forces us to eradicate the hell we create on earth by

---

[30] Laurel Schneider, *Beyond Monotheism: A Theology of Multiplicity* (New York: Routledge, 2007), 5.
[31] Lisa Isherwood, "The Embodiment of Feminist Liberation Theology: The Spiralling of Incarnation," *Feminist Theology* 12, no. 2 (2004): 140–56, quotation on 142.
[32] Ibid., 144.

instead creating heaven on earth. In this way, the political aspirations of this incarnational alternative imaginary align nicely with those of Schüssler Fiorenza's *ekklēsia of wo/men*.

In conclusion, this graduate seminar guided me further down the path of healing that I, and all of us, so desperately need. Though I didn't reach any all-encompassing solutions or universal panaceas, the seminar enabled me to analyze more deeply the ways in which kyriarchal structures have affected and continue to affect all aspects of my life. Indeed, the honesty, tenacity, passion, and activism of the other members of the seminar continue to inspire me to more fully live out a critical feminist the*logy of liberation. One of the most empowering aspects of Elisabeth Schüssler Fiorenza's work is her meticulous integration of theory and praxis. In this book, she urges us to work toward the moral affirmation all humanity's dignity, equality, and well-being. In so doing, we must actively strive toward justice for all citizens of the world. No theory of liberation is complete if it does not tangibly emancipate the communities for whom it is written. Though my healing process is not complete, because of the seminar and the insights of this book I am better equipped to help others and myself along this lifelong process.

Communicating Perceptively: What I Have Learned in Integrating Theory and Practice

Yeji Kim

As my seminar colleagues and I endeavored to bring about feminist transformations by engaging our own particularities, I determined that my area of inquiry would be the *ekklēsia of wo/men*, or the "democratic congress" of full decision-making citizens who come together to make decisions on issues pertaining to their rights and well-being. I was specifically interested in how to envision *ekklēsia* in our everyday lives, whether in our interpersonal relationships or religious communities. To me, the word *congress* meant both a formally organized space for participants to exercise their rights as full decision-making citizens, but also an informal space—the moments that wo/men with a sense of agency create in their daily lives to challenge the existing norms that deny the radical notion that "wo/men are people." The goal for me was to learn how to conjure up these almost magical moments that briefly open up *ekklēsia* and how to equip others and myself with tools to integrate these moments so that they become an essential part of our everyday lives.

But integrating my practical vision with the feminist theory we discussed in our seminar was at first daunting to me. Although *kyriarchy* in theory functions both as a deconstructive analytical tool—meaning that it can identify and name problems in a given reality—kyriarchal reality is so complex and delicate that it requires great sensitivity to human beings. This is perhaps what is most daunting about the task of deconstruction via kyriarchal analysis. We can never quite know whether the social categories we utilize—even the term *wo/men*—do justice to the particularities of each wo/man's experience.

Learning about theoretical and analytic tools such as kyriarchy and intersectionality was incredibly empowering, for they reframed my perception of the world. At the same time, the equally important insight I have gained from this seminar is how to employ these tools *perceptively*. What most helped me to overcome the fear of "incorrectly" integrating theory and practice—as to impoverish the richness of each wo/man's particularity and misrecognize their oppression—was the dialogue I had with my colleagues in the seminar and the feedback I received in the process. In response to this constructive feedback, I continued to revise my seminar paper to employ the theoretical tools *perceptively*.

I emphasize the word *perceptively* for the following reasons. As I was writing my research paper for the class, I felt dismayed in a way by the fact that no analysis of categories, no matter how extensive or thorough it may be, can fully capture the phenomenon occurring at my local church, First Korean Church in Cambridge (FKCC). My research questions for the paper were both deconstructive and reconstructive, respectively: (1) Why are wo/men in FKCC more silent than men in the Church Bible study setting? and (2) How can wo/men in FKCC envision and create moments of *ekklēsia* in these contexts? Although I was using the social categories of gender, class, race, and age for deconstruction, I was wondering to what extent these four intersectional categories accurately describe the reality. Am I, coming from a particular point of view as a mid-twenties, American-educated, and bilingual wo/man from South Korea—able to do an unbiased analysis of the phenomena at my church? Absolutely not. I learned from our seminar that no "objective" scholarship exists. Feigning "objectivity," given the power dynamics in our kyriarchal society, only means that the structures of domination are further consolidated and perpetuated in the name of the truth.

At the same time, as I was revising my draft of the paper, after receiving initial feedback from my colleagues, I felt empowered because I realized that at the heart of deconstructing a norm *perceptively* is knowing that knowledge is collective and collaborative; perceptivity results from the process of exchanging, revising, and listening with care. Deconstructive analysis, therefore, is never final, nor is it solely my knowledge. It is also this spirit of collaboration that allows us to realize *ekklēsia*.

The other challenge in this seminar was how strategically to organize grassroots movements for *ekklēsia*. As Schüssler Fiorenza mentions in this book, the Religious Right articulated an ideology of New Feminism that engendered a right-wing Roman Catholic wo/men's movement, whereas feminist struggles have become more and more limited to academic discussions. The reconstructive question for my final project (How can wo/men in FKCC envision and create the moments of *ekklēsia* in Bible study sessions?) challenged me to ponder the constructive strategies available. Two strategies that I have found useful are (1) reframing the language of *ekklēsia* in a way that it is in harmony with each culture's definition of the goal of agency, and (2) utilizing the tools of agency that wo/men in a particular culture already possess. For example, the West and the East have different conceptions of the "self": The West sees individuals as autonomous and separated from each other, whereas communal identity is more pronounced in the East. This means that the vision of *ekklēsia* for FKCC wo/men has to be in a language that is in tune with this understanding of the "self."

But what should be done when the very conception of the "self" has perpetuated kyriarchy and is the source of oppression for wo/men in FKCC? For example, this conception of the "self" in the East leads to the notion of "relationality," which means that "women's sense of self becomes very much organized around being able to make and then to maintain affiliations and relationships."[33] The notion of relationality, coupled with a Confucian understanding of wo/men's role as seeking to create harmony among relationships, is an additional *moral* pressure for FKCC wo/men. Thus, it is virtuous and mature to "not make a scene" by voicing one's opinion, since the "atmosphere" in the Bible study group clearly does not welcome wo/men's disagreement or disruption. Relationality, conscious or unconscious, is the most fundamental worldview of Korean wo/men and functions as the organizing framework from which all other subject positions arise, because it is deeply embedded in Korean culture, hence wo/men's silence in FKCC Bible studies.

However, I have learned from this seminar that each culture has its own tools with which to work in the fight against kyriarchal structures. FKCC wo/men do have one specific tool called *nun chi*, literally meaning "eye-measure." Theologian Rita Nakashima Brock describes it beautifully: "It is the ability to observe, assess, and make judgments based on a self-possessed awareness of living in multiple worlds while maintaining an attitude of concern and compassion. It is exercised by the practice of memory and reflection on values in context. It is being present while being aware of being present and examining what we *hold* together as we weave it."[34] In other words, *nun chi* is a term frequently used in Korea to describe one's ability to quickly catch what

---

[33] Simone Sunghae Kim, "Psychological Contours of Multicultural Feminist Hermeneutics: Han and Relationality," *Pastoral Psychology* 55 (2007): 723–30, quotation on 727.
[34] Rita Nakashima Brock, Jung Ha Kim, Kwok Pui-lan, and Seung Ai Yang, eds., *Off the Menu: Asian and Asian North American Women's Religion and Theology* (Louisville, KY: Westminster John Knox, 2003), 136.

the situation calls for and act in a certain way that would answer the need of the situation. The phrase *nun chi up da*, or "you have no *nun chi*" expresses that one is socially inadequate and causes a burden in a social setting. Having *nun chi*, in short, is considered a social virtue. The silence of FKCC wo/men, then, can be described as having *nun chi*. FKCC wo/men, skilled at *nun chi*, are adept at being flexible with their subject positions, "performing" multiple subject positions as the situations arise. Depending on whom they are interacting with, they quickly and almost instantly switch their subject positions.

The insight I have gained from this seminar is that the objective of *nun chi* must be framed differently: It is not only the means to merely adapt and respond to situations that call for wo/men's attention but also a tool to create opportunities to be assertive, disruptive, and even subversive, knowing that such measures, although uncomfortable in one's immediate context, can serve to build a more "open" and "inclusive" community for both wo/men and men. Honesty shown via disruption can also create an open and safe space for other women to speak their minds. Using *nun chi* to voice their opinion should be considered as an invitation toward an inclusive community, as opposed to a social burden. The insight I take from this seminar is that *nun chi* must be used not as "having" it or "not having" it, which creates the binary that those who do have it are virtuous and social, and those who do not have it are inadequate and burdensome. Instead, what is virtuous is acting freely after having considered social situations via *nun chi*.

This seminar has thus taught me how to create *ekklēsia* in our everyday lives; for me, the practice of creating *ekklēsia* in its essence is about collaboration: collaborating with others for knowledge production and collaborating with existing cultures to excavate the hidden tools for *ekklēsia* and craft it for the vision *together*. Moreover, as I was writing for this roundtable discussion, which is "a communication about the communications that have taken place in the seminar," I realized that an integral part of communicating *perceptively* when envisioning *ekklēsia* means communicating with oneself: reflecting, integrating, and synthesizing the ideas spawned around the table and the debates that took place in the seminar. This communication with oneself also works to create the space of *ekklēsia*, in which we produce new knowledge as agents of feminist transformations, to be circulated and collaborated together with knowledge produced by other agents. I invite the readers of this book to also participate in envisioning and creating the magical spaces of *ekklēsia* in our everyday lives, whether that be in a conversation with a friend, in a debate with colleagues, or just on our own comfortable couches.

Telling (Hi)stories: Feminist Theory and The*logy as a Practice of History Writing and World Making

Kelsi Morrison-Atkins

On the first page of my notes from this semester, I wrote a question—or, rather, a fragment of a question: How to tell the story of feminism in religion differently? Such shorthand, of course, engenders a number of other questions. What is "the" story of feminism in religion as it stands? What is at stake in telling the story of feminism in religion at all, let alone *differently*? Finally, and perhaps most crucially, why doesn't my question have a subject—is it I who must tell this story, or is this another's responsibility? Thus, I would like to focus on the ways in which *Congress of Wo/men: Religion, Gender, and Kyriarchal Power* addresses what it means to tell the (hi)story of feminism in religion—to tell the story of feminist scholars, activists, and practitioners struggling together, to recognize our failures, and to celebrate our successes as we imagine and enact a more just world, here and now.[35]

---

[35] By adding these parentheses to (hi)story, I hope to activate a sense that our historical reconstructions are, in many ways, *stories* based on and shaped by the encounter of our own sociopolitical contexts with those of the past. If we begin to think of historiography as a certain form of storytelling, the possibility of multiple, and perhaps even contradictory, reconstructions emerge and engage one another. Conversely, I wish also to highlight the importance of stories not as "mere fantasy" but as sites for the contestation of meaning and the negotiation of relations of power. Here, I see myself linking up with Schüssler Fiorenza's *"ekklēsia of wo/men."* She asserts, "The imaginary of *ekklesia/kosmopolis of wo/men* signifies not only fullness of being, all-encompassing inclusivity, but also dynamic multiplicity and the convergence of many different voices" (116).

As a result of our grappling together with this manuscript alongside our own scholarship in this seminar, a compelling and multivocal story of the past, present, and future of feminist theory and the*logy emerges that offers up not a single, linear trajectory of feminist studies in religion, but many mutually reinforcing (hi)stories of feminist theory and the*logy. In particular, reading this manuscript with my own explorations into feminist and queer historiography of the New Testament and Early Christianity forced me to consider the ways in which the past *matters*—that the choices made in framing and conceiving of the past have very real effects on individuals and communities in the present. Thus, a critical task of feminist theory and the*logy is to become aware of the frameworks and assumptions that shape the stories we tell. In so doing, we may become more self-reflexive (hi)story tellers as we look toward empowering wo/men in the present for our flourishing in the future.

In *Congress of Wo/men: Religion, Gender, and Kyriarchal Power*, Schüssler Fiorenza asks feminists in religion—scholars, practitioners, and those who identify as both—to come together in solidarity in the struggle against the sprawling grip of neoliberal globalization and its harmful effects on wo/men worldwide. Furthermore, she beckons feminists in the academy to take seriously the theoretical contributions of feminist scholars in religion in the service of a more just and inclusive transnational feminist landscape. To this end, Schüssler Fiorenza asserts,

> Religion and the*logy at their best cultivate the dream of a world without domination, poverty, and oppression—a dream of wellbeing and love, a dream that inspires all religions. This dream inscribed in religious scriptures becomes again and again incipient reality here and now through the struggles of sociopolitical liberation movements. In my view, feminism is such a sociopolitical movement and practice that works for a world free of dehumanizing domination compelled by the dream of a different, domination-free world (6).

Here, Schüssler Fiorenza highlights that, like religion and the*logy themselves, feminists are constantly engaged in a historically situated telling of the future—of a praxis of dreaming rooted in the present and projecting toward an already, but not yet world.[36] Such a (hi)story of feminism in religion emerges in this context as a space of and for striving, embodied activity, conflict, and community that resists a linear narrative of distinctly separable and noninteractive "waves."

The form of this book thus matches the content—feminist theorizing is brought to bear on contemporary sociopolitical circumstances, and disciplinary boundaries are transcended in the service of a feminist the*logical and political project. Here, as in all of her work, Schüssler Fiorenza narrates a (hi)story of struggle and of striving for justice in the face of kyriarchal oppression. Connecting the urgent need for dialogue between academic feminists and feminists *in* religion to our current political situation in the United States, Schüssler Fiorenza asserts, "Finally, the struggle for wo/men's reproductive rights has been declared a threat to 'religious freedom' against which conservative church leaders, such as the Roman Catholic bishops, have been fighting for the continued right to discriminate and curtail wo/men's rights. How has feminist theory responded to this sociopolitical religiously supported situation of wo/men?" (14). Such connections to the present moment, layered throughout the chapters of this book, thus serve as an incisive critique of the boundaries that would separate feminists from sharing the work of justice in the contemporary world.

Such a complex and disruptive mode of telling history—one that is charged with affect, saturated with hope, and requires active participation of body and mind—is what I brought to bear on my own experimentation with the relationship between queer and feminist

---

[36] On the *ekklēsia of wo/men* as a utopian imaginary, see Elizabeth Castelli, "The *Ekklēsia of Wo/men* and/as Utopian Space: Locating the Work of Elisabeth Schüssler Fiorenza in Feminist Utopian Thought," in *On the Cutting Edge: The Study of Women in Biblical Worlds,* eds. Jane Schaberg, Alice Bach, and Esther Fuchs (New York: Continuum, 2003), 36–52.

historiography in this course.[37] At the beginning of the semester, I stated two major goals that, at the time, I considered distinct and separable. First, I wished "to think about what it would mean to organize such a diverse community of scholars/activists/religious practitioners under the singular heading 'feminist.'" Second, I hoped to "pursue a project that will help me solidify my own methodological and historiographical investments as a scholar of New Testament and Early Christianity." As we began to discuss this manuscript as well as colleagues' work, I began to see these goals not as two "separate spheres" of action and thought, respectively, but as deeply implicated within one another. In short, I began to see how our work together became a space in which we engaged the (hi)story of feminism precisely by doing it—by struggling together with issues of globalization and economic exploitation and by offering up our own projects as potential strategies for liberation and transformation.

(Hi)story telling binds and builds community, and each of my colleagues' contributions to our discussions not only opened up for me new areas of the*logical and theoretical inquiry than I had previously been exposed to, but also invariably opened up space for central feminist questions to emerge, illuminated by the particular work of each person.[38] For instance, as we discussed the third chapter of this manuscript, "Toward a Radical Democratic Imagination: The *Ekklēsia* and *Kosmopolis*

---

[37] My investment in this critical question of the relationship between feminist and queer approaches to historiography is particularly indebted to Joseph A. Marchal, who is, to my knowledge, the first to map the interwoven trajectories of feminist and queer biblical scholars' responses to questions of the (biblical) past and our contemporary relations to/with it. See especially, Joseph A. Marchal, "Making History Queerly: Touches across Time through a Biblical Behind," *Biblical Interpretation* 19, no. 4 (2011): 373–95. In conversation with this piece, I wished to engage his "queerly feminist" approach to consider the possibilities and challenges of such a combined methodology in NT/EC studies.

[38] Of course, it would be naïve to argue that such community binding through rhetoric of history and tradition is always, or even mostly, positive and egalitarian. Rather, as Schüssler Fiorenza has argued, we must scrutinize the rhetoric that underlies every attempt at writing history and, when necessary, read against its kyriarchal and ideological grain. See, for example, Schüssler Fiorenza, *But She Said*, and Schüssler Fiorenza, *Rhetoric and Ethic*.

of Wo/men," many of us struggled with how one implements an "imaginary" and how such a utopian theoretical space might be sustained in the contemporary world. We discussed—rather, debated—whether or how these "symbolic concepts" could be implemented in the world and the ways in which the model may be susceptible to kyriarchal influence. We asked: How do we reconcile the theoretical striving for a radically democratic future with the present circumstances of injustice and disenfranchisement? How are democracy and economics related and how can we account for this in our own emancipatory imagining?

In this conversation, the line between scholar and activist lost much of its definition as we discussed the ways in which such theoretical imaginaries provide a framework for thinking about the kinds of productive possibilities for change that feminists before us have worked to cultivate and that we must carry forward in solidarity with one another.[39] Thus, unlike in many other manuscripts, in this book the work of the author is one but not the *sole* contribution to the (hi)story we tell together of feminist studies in religion. As is demonstrated throughout this metalogue, my colleagues' unique investments and frameworks of interpretation refract in a different light a number of feminist questions and also challenge my own assumptions about each of these topics.

Furthermore, each contribution to this discussion represents not an isolated intellectual endeavor, but the realized product of past feminist work and our own present visions of the future of our academic field(s), religious communities, and the sociopolitical worlds in which they are situated. As we gather around the "table" for discussion and debate—either in person or, here, in print—the assumed distinctions between thought and action as well as between past, present, and future are disrupted in each of our versions and visions of the (hi)story of feminist studies in religion.

---

[39] See the discussion of friendship and solidarity in Chapter 1 of this book.

Such spaces for debate and discussion, however, are not without disagreement, and one of the most important insights that I take away from our work together is that conflicts and disagreements, if tense, are generative and even necessary. After engaging with this text and my colleagues in this course, it is clear to me that such differences, discussions, and disagreements are the outcropping of a vision of equality that does not indicate sameness, but difference and plurivocality. As we work toward transformation of neoliberal kyriarchy, the diverse (hi)stories and structural/subject positions of wo/men around the globe are the means and motivation through which we as a global community of feminists can envision change for this world as equals, together.

Based on my experience in this course, I am thus compelled to ask: Does the story of feminist studies in religion inhere within an ethnography of wo/men in a Korean Methodist Bible study, in a sustained meditation on feminist Christology, or in the struggle for economic and ecological justice? Can the pages of a book become a vibrant site for discussion of the (hi)story of feminism—its potential in the present, and the hope it holds for a radically democratic future? As I hope the contributions to this metalogue demonstrate, the answer is a resounding "Yes!" Thus, I like to think of this book and our work together in this course as a "(hi)story of the present" that simultaneously honors and critically engages the work that has been done before, highlights the injustices and urgent needs of the present, and looks forward to a more democratic future. How do we tell the story of feminism in religion differently? We already are.

Bibliography

Abraham, Susan, and Elena Procario-Foley, eds. *Frontiers in Catholic Feminist Theology: Shoulder to Shoulder*. Minneapolis, MN: Fortress, 2009.

Achtenberg, Emily. "From Water Wars to Water Scarcity: Bolivia's Cautionary Tale." *North American Congress on Latin America NACLA*, June 5, 2013. https://nacla.org/blog/2013/6/5/water-wars-water-scarcity-bolivia's-cautionary-tale.

Agosín, Marjorie, ed. *Women, Gender, and Human Rights: A Global Perspective*. New Brunswick, NJ: Rutgers University Press, 2001.

Ahmed, Durre S., ed. *Gendering the Spirit: Women, Religion, and the Postcolonial Response* New York: Palgrave, 2002.

Allen, Amy. *The Power of Feminist Theory: Domination, Resistance, Solidarity*. Boulder: University of Colorado Press, 1999.

Althaus-Reid, Marcella, and Lisa Isherwood. *Controversies in Feminist Theologies (Controversies in Contextual Theology)*. London: SCM, 2007.

Appiah, Kwame Anthony. *Cosmopolitanism: Ethics in a World of Strangers*. New York: W. W. Norton and Co., 2006.

Aquino, María Pilar. "Theology and Identity in the Context of Globalization." In *Oxford Handbook of Feminist Theology*, edited by Mary McClintock Fulkerson and Sheila Briggs, 418–41. New York: Oxford University Press, 2011.

_____, and María José Rosado-Nunes, eds. *Feminist Intercultural Theology: Latina Explorations for a Just World*. Maryknoll, NY: Orbis Books, 2007.

Arendt, Hannah. *The Human Condition*. Chicago: University of Chicago Press, 1958.

Aristotle. *The Nicomachean Ethics: Oxford World Classics*. Translated by David Ross, Introduction by Lesley Brown. New York: Oxford University Press, 2009.

Atwood, Margaret. *The Handmaid's Tale*. New York: Ballantine, 1987.

Baker-Fletcher, Karen. *A Singing Something: Womanist Reflections on Anna Julia Cooper*. New York: Crossroad, 1994.

Baltodano, Mireya, Gabriela Miranda García, and Elisabeth Cook, eds. *Género y Religión*. San José, Costa Rica: Universidad Bíblica Latinoamericana, 2009.

Baron, Dennis. *Grammar and Gender*. New Haven, CT: Yale University Press, 1986.

Benhabib, Seyla. *Dignity in Adversity: Human Rights in Troubled Times*. Cambridge, MA: Polity, 2011.

_____. *The Reluctant Modernism of Hannah Arendt*. Thousand Oaks, CA: Sage, 1996.

Bennington, Geoffrey, and Jacques Derrida. "Politics and Friendship: A Discussion with Jacques Derrida." December 1, 1997, http://www.livingphilosophy.org/Derrida-politics-friendship.htm.

Bickford, Susan. *The Dissonance of Democracy*. Ithaca, NY: Cornell University Press, 1996.

Bornemann, Ernst. *Das Patriarchat—Ursprung und Zukunft unseres Gesellschaftssystems*. Frankfurt am Main: Fischer, 1991.

Børresen, Kari Elisabeth. *Subordination and Equivalence: The Nature and Role of Woman in Augustine and Thomas Aquinas*. Washington, DC: University Press of America, 1981.

Bourdieu, Pierre. *Masculine Domination*. Translated by Richard Nice. Stanford, CA: Stanford University Press, 2001.

Bridenthal, Renate, Anita Grossmann, and Marion Kaplan. *When Biology Became Destiny: Women in Weimar and Nazi Germany*. New York: New Feminist Library, 1984.

Briggs, Sheila, and Mary McClintock Fulkerson, eds. "Introduction." In *Oxford Handbook of Feminist Theology*, edited by Mary McClintock Fulkerson and Sheila Briggs, 1–22. New York: Oxford University Press, 2011.

Bryson, Valerie, ed. *Feminist Political Theory: An Introduction*. 2nd ed. New York: Palgrave, 2003.

Bussmann, Hadumond, and Renate Hof, eds. *Genus: Geschlechterforschung/Gender Studies in den Kultur- und Sozialwissenschaften: Ein Handbuch*. Stuttgart: A. Kröner Verlag, 2005.

Butler, Judith. *Gender Trouble: Feminism and the Subversion of Identity*. New York: Routledge, 1990.

_____. *Undoing Gender*. New York: Routledge, 2004.

_____, and Joan W. Scott, eds. *Feminists Theorize the Political*. New York: Routledge, 1992.

Carter, Jimmy. *A Call to Action: Women, Religion, Violence, and Power*. New York: Simon and Schuster, 2014.

Castelli, Elizabeth A. "The *Ekklēsia* of Wo/men and/as Utopian Space: Locating the Work of Elisabeth Schüssler Fiorenza in Feminist Utopian Thought." In *On the Cutting Edge: The Study of Women in Biblical Worlds*, edited by Jane Schaberg, Alice Bach, and Esther Fuchs, 26–52. New York: Continuum, 2003.

_____, ed. *Women, Gender, and Religion: A Reader*. New York: Palgrave, 2001.

Chopp, Rebecca S. *The Power to Speak: Feminism, Language, and God*. New York: Crossroad, 1989.

Clifford, Anne M. *Introducing Feminist Theology*. Maryknoll, NY: Orbis, 2001.

Cocks, Joan. *The Oppositional Imagination: Feminism, Critique, and Political Theory*. New York: Routledge, 1989.

Code, Lorraine. "Patriarchy." In *Encyclopedia of Feminist Theories*, edited by Lorraine Code, 378–79. London: Routledge, 2000.

Cohen, Nancy L. *Delirium: How the Sexual Counterrevolution Is Polarizing America: A Groundbreaking Investigation into the Shadow Movement that Fuels Our Political Wars*. Berkeley, CA: Counterpoint, 2012.

Colbert Report. "June 27, 2012." The Colbert Report video, 6:41. June 27, 2012. http://www.cc.com/episodes/huq5u6/the-colbert-report-june-27—2012—-melinda-gates-season-8-ep-08119.

Conde, Gloria. Mujer nueva: Ellas: Hay una pequena diferencia. *Translated by Karna Swanson. New York: Circle Press, 2002.*

Cornwall, Andrea, Jasmine Gideon, and Kalpana Wilson. "Introduction: Reclaiming Feminism: Gender and Neoliberalism." *IDS Bulletin* 39, no. 6 (2008): 1–9.

Cornwall, Susannah. "Sex Otherwise: Intersex, Christology, and the Maleness of Jesus," *Journal of Feminist Studies in Religion* 30, no. 2 (2014): 23–39.

Covert, Bryce. "Melissa Harris-Perry on the Politics and Pitfalls of Motherhood in America." *Think Progress,* last modified March 10, 2014, http://thinkprogress.org/economy/2014/03/10/3382941/ mhp-motherhood/.

Daly, Mary. *Beyond God the Father.* Boston: Beacon, 1984.

De Lauretis, Teresa. *Technologies of Gender.* Bloomington: Indiana University Press, 1987.

DeFranza, Megan K. *Sex Difference in Christian Theology: Male, Female, and Intersex in the Image of God.* Grand Rapids, MI: Eerdmans, 2015.

Delphy, Christine. "Rethinking Sex and Gender." In Juschka, *Feminism in the Study of Religion,* 411–23.

DiStephano, Christine. *Configurations of Masculinity: A Feminist Perspective on Modern Political Theory.* Ithaca, NY: Cornell University Press, 1991.

Doetsch-Kidder, Sharon. *Social Change and Intersectional Activism: The Spirit of Social Movement.* New York: Palgrave MacMillan, 2012.

Doyle, Karen. *The Genius of Womanhood.* Boston, MA: Pauline Books and Media, 2009.

Drake, Tim. "Teaching John Paul II's 'New Feminism'—1 Woman at a Time." *National Catholic Register,* March 10, 2011. http://www.ncregister.com/daily-news/teaching-john-paul-iis-new-feminism-1-woman-at-a-time#ixzz1zlCq6ZJT.

DuBois, Page. *Centaurs and Amazons: Women and the Pre-History of the Great Chain of Being*. Ann Arbor: University of Michigan Press, 1982.

_____. *Torture and Truth*. London: Routledge, 1991.

Duggan, Lisa. *The Twilight of Equality: Neoliberalism, Cultural Politics, and the Attack on Democracy*. Boston: Beacon, 2003.

Durish, Patricia. *Citizenship and Difference: Feminist Debates*. Annotated Bibliographies Series of the Transformative Learning Centre. Toronto: Ontario Institute for Studies in Education, 2002.

Epps, Garrett. "What Makes Indiana's Religious Freedom Law Different?" *The Atlantic*, March 30, 2015. http://www.theatlantic.com/politics/archive/2015/03/what-makes-indianas-religious-freedom-law-different/388997/.

Evans, Mary. "Feminism and the Implications of Austerity." *Feminist Review* 109 (2015): 146–55.

Farley, Margaret A. *Just Love: A Framework for Christian Sexual Ethics*. New York: Continuum, 2006.

Faure, Christine. *Democracy without Women: Feminism and the Rise of Liberal Individualism in France*. Bloomington: Indiana University Press, 1991.

Fausto-Sterling, Anne. *Sexing the Body: Gender Politics and the Construction of Sexuality*. New York: Basic Books, 2000.

Feldman, Shelley. "Exploring Theories of Patriarchy: A Perspective from Contemporary Bangladesh." *Signs* 26, no. 4 (2001): 1097–127.

Fernandes, Leela. *Transforming Feminist Practice: Non-Violence, Social Justice, and the Possibility of a Spiritualized Feminism*. San Francisco: Aunt Lute, 2003.

Foss, Karen A., Sonja K. Foss, and Cindy L. Griffin. *Feminist Rhetorical Theories*. Thousand Oaks, CA: Sage, 1999.

Fox Genovese, Elizabeth. Feminism Is Not the Story of My Life: How Today's Feminist Elite Has Lost Touch with the Real Concerns of Women. *New York:* Doubleday, 1996.

Frank Parsons, Susan. *The Cambridge Companion to Feminist Theology*. New York: Cambridge University Press, 2002.

Fraser, Nancy. *Fortunes of Feminism: From State-Managed Capitalism to Neoliberal Crisis.* London: Verso, 2013.

_____. "How Feminism Became Capitalism's Handmaiden and How to Reclaim It." *The Guardian,* October 14, 2013. http://www.theguardian.com/commentisfree/2013/oct/14/feminism-capitalist-handmaiden-neoliberal.

_____. "Identity, Exclusion, and Critique: A Response to Four Critics." *European Journal of Political Theory* 6, no. 3 (2005): 305–38.

_____. "Mapping the Feminist Imagination: From Redistribution to Recognition to Representation." *Constellations* 12, no. 3 (2005): 295–307.

Gebara, Ivone. *Longing for Running Water: Ecofeminism and Liberation.* Minneapolis, MN: Fortress, 1999.

_____. *Out of the Depth: Women's Experience of Evil and Salvation.* Minneapolis, MN: Fortress, 2002.

Giroux, Henry A. "Donald Trump and the Ghost of Totalitarianism." September 9, 2015. http://www.tikkun.org/nextgen/donald-trump-and-the-ghost-of-totalitarianism.

Goss, Robert. *Queering Christ: Beyond "Jesus Acted Up."* Cleveland, OH: Pilgrim, 2002.

Grewal, Inderpal. *Transnational America: Feminisms, Diasporas, Neoliberalisms.* Durham, NC: Duke University Press, 2005.

Gross, Melanie, and Gabriele Winkler, eds. *Queer-, Feministische Kritiken neoliberaler Verhältnisse.* Münster: Unrast, 2007.

Gross, Rita M., and Rosemary Radford Ruether. *Religious Feminism and the Future of the Planet: A Buddhist-Christian Conversation.* New York: Continuum, 2001.

Gunn Allen, Paula. *The Sacred Hoop: Recovering the Feminine in American Indian Traditions.* Boston: Beacon, 1986.

Gupta, Rahila. "Has Neoliberalism Knocked Feminism Sideways?" *50.50 Inclusive Democracy,* January 4, 2012. https://www.opendemocracy.net/5050/rahila-gupta/has-neoliberalism-knocked-feminism-sideways.

Hall, Lee. "I Am an Adjunct Professor Who Teaches Five Classes and I Earn Less Than a Pet-Sitter," *The Guardian,* June 23, 2015.

http://www.theguardian.com/commentisfree/2015/jun/22/adjunct-professor-earn-less-than-pet-sitter.

Harvey, David. *A Brief History of Neoliberalism*. Oxford: Oxford University Press, 2005.

Hawkesworth, Mary E. *Beyond Oppression: Feminist Theory and Political Strategy*. New York: Continuum, 1990.

_____. *Globalization and Feminist Activism*. Lanham, MD: Rowman & Littlefield, 2006.

Hawley, John Stratton, ed. *Fundamentalism and Gender*. New York: Oxford University Press, 1994.

Hekman, Susan. *The Feminine Subject*. Cambridge: Polity Press, 2014.

Helman, Ivy A. *Women and the Vatican: An Exploration of Official Documents*. New York: Orbis, 2012.

Hemmings, Clare. *Why Stories Matter: The Political Grammar of Feminist Theory*. Durham, NC: Duke University Press, 2011.

Hennessy, Rosemary. *Materialist Feminism and the Politics of Discourse*. New York: Routledge, 1993.

Hernández, Adriana. *Pedagogy, Democracy, and Feminism: Rethinking the Public Sphere*. New York: SUNY Press, 1997.

Hilkert Andolsen, Barbara. *Daughters of Jefferson, Daughters of Bootblacks: Racism and American Feminism*. Macon, GA: Mercer, 1986.

Hill Collins, Patricia. *Fighting Words: Black Women and the Search for Justice*. Minneapolis: University of Minnesota Press, 1998.

_____. *On Intellectual Activism*. Philadelphia: Temple University Press, 2013.

Holmes, Mary. *What Is Gender? Sociological Approaches*. Thousand Oaks, CA: Sage, 2007.

Honig, Bonnie, ed. *Feminist Interpretations of Hannah Arendt*. University Park: Pennsylvania University Press, 1995.

hooks, bell. *Feminism Is For Everybody: Passionate Politics*. Cambridge, MA: South End, 2000.

_____. *Yearning: Race, Gender, and Cultural Politics*. Boston, MA: South End, 1990.

Horkheimer, Max. *Critical Theory*. New York: Herder, 1972.

Isherwood, Lisa. "The Embodiment of Feminist Liberation Theology: The Spiralling of Incarnation." *Feminist Theology* 12, no. 2 (2004): 140–56.

Jarl, Ann-Cathrin. *In Justice: Women and Global Economics*. Minneapolis, MN: Fortress, 2003.

John Paul II. "Apostolic Letter on the Dignity and Vocation of Women *Mulieris Dignitatem*." Vatican Website, August 15, 1988. http://w2.vatican.va/content/john-paul-ii/en/apost_letters/1988/documents/hf_jp-ii_apl_19880815_mulieris-dignitatem.html.

_____. *Evangelium Vitae*. The Vatican Website, March 25, 1995. http://w2.vatican.va/content/john-paul-ii/en/encyclicals/documents/hf_jp-ii_enc_25031995_evangelium-vitae.html.

_____. "Letter of Pope John Paul II to Women." The Vatican Website, June 29, 1995. https://w2.vatican.va/content/john-paul-ii/en/letters/1995/documents/hf_jp-ii_let_29061995_women.html.

Johnson, Elizabeth. "Redeeming the Name of Christ." In *Freeing Theology: The Essentials of Theology in Feminist Perspective*, edited by Catherine Mowry LaCugna, 115–27. San Francisco, CA: HarperSanFrancisco, 1993.

_____. *She Who Is: The Mystery of God in Feminist Theological Discourse*. New York: Crossroad, 1992.

_____. *Truly Our Sister: A Theology of Mary in the Communion of Saints*. New York: Continuum, 2003.

Joice, Kathryn. *Quiverfull: Inside the Christian Patriarchy Movement*. Boston: Beacon, 2009.

Juschka, Darlene, ed. *Feminism in the Study of Religion: A Reader*. New York: Continuum, 2001.

Kähler, Else. *Die Frau in den Paulinischen Briefen*. Zürich: Gotthelf Verlag, 1960.

Kalbian, Aline H. *Sexing the Church: Gender, Power, and Ethics in Contemporary Catholicism*. Bloomington: Indiana University Press, 2005.

Kamitsuka, Margaret D. *Feminist Theology and the Challenge of Difference*. New York: Oxford University Press, 2007.

Kang, Namsoon. *Diasporic Feminist Theology: Asia and the Theopolitical Imagination*. Minneapolis, MN: Fortress, 2014.

Kanyoro, Musimbi R. A. *Introducing Feminist Cultural Hermeneutics: An African Perspective*. Cleveland, OH: Pilgrim Press, 2002.

Kassian, Mary. *The Feminist Mistake: The Radical Impact of Feminism and Culture*. 2nd ed. Wheaton, IL: Crossway, 2005.

Keating, Cricket. "Building Coalitional Consciousness." *NWSA Journal* 17, no. 2 (2005): 86–103.

Keuls, Eva C. *The Reign of the Phallus: Sexual Politics in Ancient Athens*. Berkeley: University of California Press, 1993.

Kleingeld, Pauline, and Eric Brown. "Cosmopolitantism." *Stanford Encyclopedia of Philosophy*, edited by Edward N. Zalta. Fall 2014. http://plato.stanford.edu/entries/cosmopolitanism.

Klitgaard, Kent A., and Lisi Krall, "Ecological Economics, Degrowth, and Institutional Change." *Ecological Economics* 84, no. 1 (2012): 247–53.

Kohrs Campbell, Karlyn. "Consciousness-Raising: Linking Theory, Criticism, and Practice." *Rhetoric Society Quarterly* 32, no. 1 (2002): 45–64.

Koonz, Claudia. *Mothers in the Fatherland: Women, the Family, and Nazi Politics*. New York: Routledge, 1986.

Kraut, Richard. "Aristotle's Ethics." In *Stanford Encyclopedia of Philosophy*, edited by Edward N. Zalta. Summer 2014. http://plato.stanford.edu/entries/aristotle-ethics/.

Kwok Pui-lan. *Postcolonial Imagination and Feminist Theology*. Louisville, KY: Westminster John Knox, 2005.

Laqueur, Thomas. *Making Sex: Body and Gender from the Greeks to Freud*. Cambridge, MA: Harvard University Press, 1990.

Lara, Irene. "Latina Health Activist-Healers Bridging Body and Spirit." *Women and Therapy* 31, no. 1(2008): 21–40.

Lewis, Reina, and Sara Mills, eds. *Feminist Postcolonial Theory: A Reader*. New York: Routledge, 2003.

Lewis, William. "Louis Althusser." In *The Stanford Encyclopedia of Philosophy*, edited by Edward N. Zalta. Spring 2014. http://plato.stanford.edu/archives/spr2014/entries/althusser.

Lloyd, Genevieve. *The Man of Reason: "Male" and "Female" in Western Philosophy*. Minneapolis: University of Minnesota Press, 1984.

Lorber, Judith. *Paradoxes of Gender*. New Haven, CT: Yale University Press, 1994.

Lucal, Betsy. "What It Means to Be Gendered Me: Life on the Boundaries of a Dichotomous Gender System." *Gender and Society* 13, no. 6 (1999): 781–97.

Lugones, María. "Heterosexualism and the Colonial/Modern Gender System." *Hypatia* 22, no. 1 (2007): 186–209.

———. "Toward a Decolonial Feminism." *Hypatia* 25, no. 4 (2010): 742–59.

Lührmann, Dieter. "Woman nicht mehr Sklave und Freier ist: Überlegungen zur Struktur frühchristlicher Gemeinden." *Wort und Dienst* 13 (1975): 53–83.

Lutz, Helma, Maria Theresa Herrera Vivar, and Linda Supik, eds. *Focus Intersektionalität: Bewegungen und Verortungen eines vielschichtigen Konzepts*. Wiesbaden: VS Verlag, 2010.

Lykke, Nina. *Feminist Studies: A Guide to Intersectional Theory, Methodology, and Writing*. New York: Routledge, 2010.

Lynch, Sandra. "Aristotle and Friendship." *Contretemps* 3 (July 2002): 98–108.

Lyndon Shanley, Mary, and Carol Pateman, eds. *Feminist Interpretations and Political Theory*. Cambridge: Polity, 1991.

Macleod, Morna. "Drawing the Connection: Mayan Women's Quest for a Gendered Spirituality." In *Women and Indigenous Religions*, edited by Sylvia Marcos, 195–215. Santa Barbara, CA: Praeger, 2010.

Manning, Christel. *God Gave Us the Right: Conservative Catholic, Evangelical Protestant, and Orthodox Jewish Women Grapple with Feminism*. New Brunswick, NJ: Rutgers University Press, 1999.

Marchal, Joseph A. "Making History Queerly: Touches across Time through a Biblical Behind." *Biblical Interpretation* 19, no. 4 (2011): 373–95.

Marcos, Sylvia. "Indigenous Spirituality and the Politics of Justice: Voices from the First Summit of Indigenous Women of the Americas." In *Women and Indigenous Religions*, edited by Sylvia Marcos, 45–68. Santa Barbara, CA: Praeger, 2010.

Martin, Clarice. "The *Haustafeln* Household Codes in African American Biblical Interpretation: 'Free Slaves' and 'Subordinate Women.'" In *Stony the Road We Trod: African American Biblical Interpretation*, edited by Cain Hope Felder, 206–31. Minneapolis, MN: Fortress, 1991.

May, Todd. *Friendship in an Age of Economics: Resisting the Force of Neoliberalism*. Lanham, MD: Lexington, 2012.

McCarthy Brown, Karen. "Fundamentalism and the Control of Women." In *Fundamentalism and Gender*, edited by John Stratton Hawley, 175–201. New York: Oxford University Press, 1994.

McClintock, Anne. *Imperial Leather: Race, Gender, and Sexuality in the Colonial Contest*. London: Routledge, 1995.

_____, Aamir Mufti, and Ella Shohat, eds. *Dangerous Liaisons: Gender, Nation, and Postcolonial Perspectives*. Minneapolis: University of Minnesota Press, 1997.

McCulley, Carolyn. *Radical Womanhood: Feminine Faith in a Feminist World*. Chicago: Moody, 2008.

McGowan, John. *Hannah Arendt: An Introduction*. Minneapolis: University of Minnesota Press, 1998.

Meyer-Wilmes, Hedwig. "The Diversity of Ministry in a Postmodern Church." In *The Non-Ordination of Women and the Politics of Power*, edited by Elisabeth Schüssler Fiorenza and Hermann Häring, 69–88. Maryknoll, NY: Orbis, 1999.

Mies, Maria. *Patriarchy and Accumulation on a World Scale: Women in the International Division of Labour*. New York: Palgrave, 1999.

Miller, Anna C. *Corinthian Democracy: Democratic Discourse in 1 Corinthians*. Eugene, OR: Pickwick, 2015.

Miller, Patricia. *Good Catholics: The Battle over Abortion in the Catholic Church*. Berkeley: University of California Press, 2014.

Mitchem, Stephanie Y. *Introducing Womanist Theology*. Maryknoll, NY: Orbis Books, 2002.

Moghadam, Valentine M. *Globalization and Social Movements: Islamism, Feminism, and the Global Justice Movement*. 2nd ed. Lanham, MD: Rowman & Littlefield, 2013.

Mohanty, Chandra Talpade. "Under Western Eyes." In *Third World Women and the Politics of Feminism*, edited by Chandra Talpade Mohanty, Ann Russo, and Lourdes Torres, 51–80. Bloomington: Indiana University Press, 1991.

Moller Okin, Susan. *Women in Western Political Thought*. Princeton, NJ: Princeton University Press, 1979.

Mookherjee, Monika. "Affective Citizenship: Feminism, Postcolonialism, and the Politics of Recognition." *Critical Review of International Social and Political Philosophy* 8, no. 1 (2005): 31–50.

Moore, Stephen D., and Janice Capel Anderson, eds. *New Testament Masculinities*. Semeia Studies. Atlanta: SBL, 2003.

Nakashima Brock, Rita, Jung Ha Kim, Kwok Pui-lan, and Seung Ai Yang, eds. *Off the Menu: Asian and Asian North American Women's Religion and Theology*. Louisville, KY: Westminster John Knox, 2007.

Nanda, Serena. *Gender Diversity: Crosscultural Variations*. 2nd ed. Long Grove, IL: Waveland Press, 2014.

Nash, Jennifer C. "Rethinking Intersectionality." *Feminist Review* 89, no. 1 (2008): 1–15.

Ng, Esther Yue L. *Reconstructing Christian Origins? The Feminist Theology of Elisabeth Schüssler Fiorenza: An Evaluation*. Carlisle, PA: Paternoster, 2002.

Nicholson, Linda J. *Feminism/Postmodernism*. New York: Routledge, 1990.

Oakley, Ann. *Sex, Gender, and Society*. New York: Harper & Row, 1972.

Omang, Joanne. "Playing Hardball against Women's Rights: The Holy See at the UN." *Conscience* 34, no. 2 (November 2, 2013). http://churchandstate.org.uk/2013/08/playing-hardball-against-womens-rights-the-holy-see-at-the-un/.

Oyewùmi, Oyéronké. *The Invention of Women: Making an African Sense of Western Gender Discourses*. Minneapolis: University of Minnesota Press, 1997.

Paden, William E. *Religious Worlds: The Comparative Study of Religion*. Boston: Beacon, 1994.

Padgett, Tim. "Sorry, Rome, U.S. Catholics Are More Like Melinda Gates." *Time*, July 12, 2012. http://ideas.time.com/2012/07/12/sorry-rome-us-catholics-more-like-melinda-gates/?iid=op-article-mostpop1#ixzz20XJaRjpi.

Paltrow, Lynn M., and Jeanne Flavin. "Pregnant, and No Civil Rights." *New York Times*, November 7, 2014. http://www.nytimes.com/ 2014/11/08/opinion/pregnant-and-no-civil-rights.html.

Paul VI. *Lumen Gentium*. The Vatican Website, November 21, 1964. http://www.vatican.va/archive/hist_councils/ii_vatican_council/documents/vat-ii_const_19641121_lumen-gentium_en.html.

Perinfalvi, Rita, ed. *Women and Religion: Dignity of the Woman as Dignity of the Human Being*. Cluj-Napoca: Verbum, 2011.

Phillips, Anne. *Engendering Democracy*. University Park: University of Pennsylvania Press, 1991.

Plaskow, Judith. *Sex, Sin, and Grace: Women's Experience and the Theologies of Niebuhr and Tillich*. Washington, DC: University Press of America, 1980.

_____. *Standing Again at Sinai: Judaism from a Feminist Perspective*. New York: HarperCollins, 1991.

Pogge, Thomas, and Winfried Menko. "Cosmopolitanism and Sovereignty." In *World Poverty and Human Rights: Cosmopolitan Responsibilities and Reforms*. Cambridge: Polity, 2002.

Prins, Baukje. "Mothers and Muslims, Sisters and Sojourners: The Contested Boundaries of Feminist Citizenship." In *Handbook of*

    Gender and Women's Studies, edited by Kathy Davis, Mary Evans, and Judith Lorber, 234–50. London: Sage, 2006.

Radford Ruether, Rosemary. *Christianity and the Making of the Modern Family*. Boston: Beacon, 2000.

_____, ed. *Feminist Theologies: Legacy and Prospect*. Minneapolis, MN: Fortress, 2007.

_____. *Catholic Does Not Equal the Vatican: A Vision for Progressive Catholicism*. New York: The New Press, 2008.

_____. "Patriarchy." In *An A to Z of Feminist Theology*, edited by Lisa Isherwood and Dorothea McEwan, 173–74. Sheffield: Sheffield Academic Press, 1996.

_____. *Women Healing the Earth: Third World Women on Ecology, Feminism, and Religion*. Maryknoll, NY: Orbis, 1996.

Ramey Molenkott, Virginia. "Emancipative Elements in Ephesians 5, 21–33: Why Feminist Scholarship Has Often Left Them Unmentioned, and Why They Should Be Emphasized." In *A Feminist Companion to the Deutero-Pauline Epistles*, edited by Amy-Jill Levine, 37–58. New York: Continuum, 2003.

_____. *Omnigender: A Trans-religious Approach*. Cleveland, OH: Pilgrim, 2001.

_____. *Women, Men, and the Bible*. Nashville, TX: Abingdon, 1977.

Raphael, Melissa. *Introducing Thealogy: Discourse on the Goddess*. Cleveland, OH: Pilgrim Press, 2000.

Rebeka Anic, Jadranka. "Gender Politik und die Katholische Kirche." In *Feminist Theology in Europe: A Reader in Honor of Hedwig Meyer-Wilmes*, edited by Elzbieta Adamiak and Marie Theres Wacker, 64–79. Münster: LIT Verlag, 2013.

Reilly, Niamh. "Cosmopolitan Feminism and Human Rights." *Hypatia* 22, no. 4 (2007):180–98.

Ress, Mary Judith. *Ecofeminism in Latin America*. Maryknoll, NY: Orbis, 2006.

Riesman, Barbara J. "Gender as Social Structure: Theory Wrestling with Activism." In *The Kaleidoscope of Gender: Prisms, Patterns, and Possibilities*, edited by Joan Z. Spade and Catherine G. Valentine, 9–21. Thousand Oaks, CA: Sage, 2007.

Ross, Tamar. *Expanding the Palace of Torah: Orthodoxy and Feminism.* Lebanon, NH: University Press of New England, 2004.

Rouselle, Aline. *Porneia: On Desire and the Body in Antiquity.* New York: Basil Blackwell, 1988.

Roy, Arundhati. *An Ordinary Person's Guide to Empire.* Cambridge, MA: South End, 2004.

Sandoval, Chela. *Methodology of the Oppressed.* Minneapolis: University of Minnesota Press, 2000.

Scanzoni, Letha, and Nancy Hardesty. *All We're Meant to Be: A Biblical Approach to Women's Liberation.* Waco, TX: Word Books, 1975.

Schäfer-Bossert, Stefanie, and Elisabeth Hartlieb. *Feministische Theologie-Politische Theologie: Entwicklungen und Perspektiven.* Sulzbach: Ulrike Helmer Verlag, 2012.

Schnabl, Christa. *Hannah Arendts Theorie des Handelns im Horizont der theologischen Ethik.* Frankfurt: P. Lang, 1999.

Schneider, Laurel. *Beyond Monotheism: A Theology of Multiplicity.* New York: Routledge, 2007.

Scholer, David M. "Tim 2:9–15 and the Place of Women in the Church's Ministry." In *Feminist Companion to the Deutero-Pauline Epistles,* edited by Amy-Jill Levine, 98–121. New York: Continuum, 2003.

Scholz, Susanne. "The Christian Rights Discourse on Gender and the Bible." *Journal of Feminist Studies in Religion* 21.1 (2005): 81–100.

———. "The Forbidden Fruit for the New Eve: The Christian Right's Adaptation to the Post Modern World." In *Interreligious Hermeneutics in Pluralistic Europe: Between Texts and People,* edited by David Cheetham, Ulrich Winkler, Oddbjørn Lirvik, and Juditth Gruber, 289–315. Amsterdam: Odopi, 2011.

Schor, Naomi, and Elizabeth Weed, eds. *The Essential Difference.* Bloomington: Indiana University Press, 1994.

Schott, Robin May. *Cognition and Eros: A Critique of the Kantian Paradigm.* Boston: Beacon, 1988.

Schumacher, Michele M., ed. *Women in Christ: Toward a New Feminism*. Grand Rapids, MI: Eerdmans, 2003.

Schüssler Fiorenza, Elisabeth. *But She Said: Feminist Practices of Biblical Interpretation*. Boston: Beacon, 1992.

_____. *Changing Horizons: Explorations in Feminist Interpretation*. Minneapolis, MN: Fortress Press, 2013.

_____. "Critical Feminist The*logy of Liberation: A Decolonizing Political The*logy." In *Political Theology: Contemporary Challenges and Future Directions*, edited by Francis Schüssler Fiorenza, Klaus Tanner, and Michael Welker, 23–26. Louisville, KY: Westminster John Knox, 2013.

_____. *Democratizing Biblical Studies: Toward an Emancipatory Educational Space*. Louisville: Westminster John Knox, 2009.

_____. *Discipleship of Equals: A Critical Feminist Ekklesia-logy of Liberation*. New York: Crossroad, 1993.

_____. *Empowering Memory and Movement: Thinking and Working Across Borders*. Minneapolis, MN: Fortress Press, 2013.

_____. *Feminist Biblical Studies in the Twentieth Century: Scholarship and Movement*. Minneapolis, MN: Fortress Press, 2013.

_____. "Gender, Sprache, und Religion: Feministisch–Theologische Anfragen." In *Erträge. 60 Jahre Augustana*, 83-90. Neuendettelsau: Augustana Hochschule e.V., 2008.

_____. *In Memory of Her: A Feminist Theological Reconstruction of Christian Origins*. New York: Crossroad, 1983.

_____. *Los Caminos de la Sabiduria: Una Introducción a la interpretación feminista de la Biblia*. Santander, Spain: Sal Terrae, 2004.

_____. "Poder, Diversidad y Religión." Special Issue of *La Revista Vida y Pensamiento* 32, no. 2 (2013).

_____. "The Power of the Word: Charting Critical Global Feminist Biblical Studies." In *Feminist New Testament Studies: Global and Future Perspectives*, edited by Kathleen O'Brien Wicker, Althea Spencer Miller, and Musa W. Dube, 43–62. New York: Palgrave MacMillan, 2005.

_____. *The Power of the Word: Scripture and the Rhetoric of Empire*. Minneapolis, MN: Fortress Press, 2007.

_____. "Religion, Gender, and Society: Shaping the Discipline of Religious/Theological Studies." In *The Relevance of Theology*, edited by Carl Reinhold Bråckenhielm and Gunhild Winqvist Hollman, 85–99. Uppsala, Sweden: Uppsala Universitet, 2002.

_____. *Rhetoric and Ethic: The Politics of Biblical Studies*. Minneapolis, MN: Fortress, 1999.

_____. "Toward an Intersectional Analytic: Race, Gender, Ethnicity, and Empire in Early Christian Studies." In *Prejudice and Christian Beginnings*, edited by Laura Nasrallah and Elisabeth Schüssler Fiorenza, 1–26. Minneapolis, MN: Fortress, 2009.

_____. *Transforming Vision: Explorations in Feminist The*logy*. Minneapolis, MN: Fortress, 2011.

_____. *Wisdom Ways: Introducing Feminist Biblical Interpretation*. Maryknoll, NY: Orbis Books, 2001.

_____, Karen Derris, Rachel Adelman, Karen Pechilis, and Aysha Hidayatullah. "Special Section: Comparative Feminist Hermeneutics." *Journal of Feminist Studies in Religion* 30, no. 2 (2014): 57–129.

Sing, Shweta. "Global Feminism." In *Encyclopedia of Women in Today's World*, edited by Mary Zeiss Stange, Carol K. Oyster, and Jene E. Sloane, 628–30. Thousand Oaks, CA: Sage, 2011.

Smith, Andrea. "First Nation, Empire, and Globalization." In *Oxford Handbook of Feminist Theology*, edited by Mary McClintock Fulkerson and Sheila Briggs, 307–21. New York: Oxford University Press, 2011.

Smith, Anne Marie. *Laclau, and Mouffe: The Radical Democratic Imaginary*. New York: London, 1998.

Sommerbauer, Jutta. *Differenzen Zwischen Frauen: Zur Positionsbestimmung und Kritik des Postmodernen Feminismus*. Münster: Unrast, 2003.

Sowards, Stacy K., and Valerie R. Renegar. "The Rhetorical Functions of Consciousness Raising in Third Wave Feminism." *Communication Studies* 55, no. 4 (2005): 535–52.

Spahic-Siljak, Zilka, ed. *Contesting Female, Feminist and Muslim Identities: Post-Socialist Contexts of Bosnia and Herzegovina and Kosovo.*

Sarajevo: Center for Interdisciplinary Postgraduate Studies, 2012.

Spivak, Gayatri Chakravorty. "Can the Subaltern Speak?" In *Marxism and the Interpretation of Culture*, edited by Cary Nelson and Lawrence Grossberg, 271–97. Urbana: University of Illinois Press, 1988.

Staller, Karen. "Metalogue as Methodology." *Qualitative Social Work* 6, no. 2 (2007): 137–57.

Standing, Guy. "Global Feminization through Flexible Labor." *World Development* 17.7 (1989): 1077–95.

Stoljar, Natalie. "Essentialism." In Code, *Encyclopedia of Feminist Theories*, 177–78.

Sunghae Kim, Simone. "Psychological Contours of Multicultural Feminist Hermeneutics: Han and Relationality." *Pastoral Psychology* 55 (2007): 723–30.

Syme, Ronald. *The Roman Revolution*. Oxford: Oxford University Press, 1939.

Taylor, Laura. "Redeeming Christ: Imitation or ReCitation?" In *Frontiers in Catholic Feminist Theology: Shoulder to Shoulder*, edited by Susan Abraham and Elena Procario-Foley, 119–40. Minneapolis, MN: Fortress, 2009.

Thistlethwaite, Susan Brooks. *Women's Bodies as Battlefields: Christian Theology and the Global War on Women*. New York: Palgrave Macmillan, 2015.

Thompson, John B. *Studies in the Theory of Ideology*. Cambridge: Polity, 1984.

Thraede, Klaus. "Aerger mit der Freiheit: Die Bedeutung von Frauen in Theorie und Praxis der alten Kirche." In *"Freunde in Christus werden ...": die Beziehung von Mann und Frau als Frage an Theologie und Kirche*, edited by Gerda Scharffenroth and Klaus Thraede, 35–182. Gelnhausen and Berlin: Burckhardthaus, 1977.

Valencia Sáiz, Angel. "Globalization, Cosmopolitanism, and Ecological Citizenship." *Environmental Politics* 14, no. 2 (2005): 163–78.

Vogue, Ariane, and Jeremy Diamond. "Supreme Court Rules in Favor of Same-Sex Marriage Nationwide." *CNN*, June 27, 2015, http://www.cnn.com/2015/06/26/politics/supreme-court-same-sex-marriage-ruling/.

Walby, Sylvia. *Theorizing Patriarchy*. Oxford: Basil, 1990.

Walker, Alice. *In Search of Our Mothers' Gardens: Womanist Prose*. San Diego, CA: Harcourt Brace Jovanovich, 1983.

Weber, Lynn. *Understanding Race, Class, Gender, and Sexuality: A Conceptual Framework*. 2nd ed. New York: Oxford University Press, 2010.

Weedon, Chris. *Feminist Practice and Poststructuralist Theory*. Malden, MA: Blackwell, 1987.

Welker, Michael, ed. *Quest for Freedom: Biblical-Historical-Contemporary*. Neukirchen-Vluyn: Neukirchener Verlag, 2015.

Wichterich, Christa. *The Globalized Woman: Reports from a Future of Inequality*. New York: Zed, 2000.

Wildung Harrison, Beverly. *Justice in the Making: Feminist Social Ethics*. Louisville, KY: Westminster John Knox, 2004.

Williams Crenshaw, Kimberlé. "Mapping the Margins: Intersectionality, Identity Politics, and Violence against Women of Color." In *The Feminist Philosophy Reader*, edited by Alison Bailey and Chris Cuomo, 279–309. New York: McGraw-Hill, 2008.

Winker, Gabriele, and Nina Degele. *Intersektionalität. Zur Analyse sozialer Ungleichheiten*. Bielefeld: Transcript, 2009.

Wollrad, Eske. *Weisssein im Widerspruch: Feministische Perspektiven auf Rassismus, Kultur, und Religion*. Königstein/Taunus: Helmer, 2005.

Yamaguchi, Satoko. "Father Image of God and Inclusive Language: A Reflection in Japan." In *Toward a New Heaven and Earth: Essays in Honor of Elisabeth Schüssler Fiorenza*, edited by Fernando Segovia, 198–224. Maryknoll, NY: Orbis, 2003.

Zerilli, Linda M. G. *Feminism and the Abyss of Freedom*. Chicago: University of Chicago Press, 2005.

Zevallos, Zuleya. "What Is Otherness?" *Other Sociologist*, June 6, 2015. http://othersociologist.com/otherness-resources/.

www.ingramcontent.com/pod-product-compliance
Lightning Source LLC
Chambersburg PA
CBHW061738270326
41928CB00011B/2286